HIS HANDS
Resources for Lent and Easter

edited by
Jon L. Joyce

HIS HANDS

PRINTED IN U.S.A.

TABLE OF CONTENTS

Preaching Resources

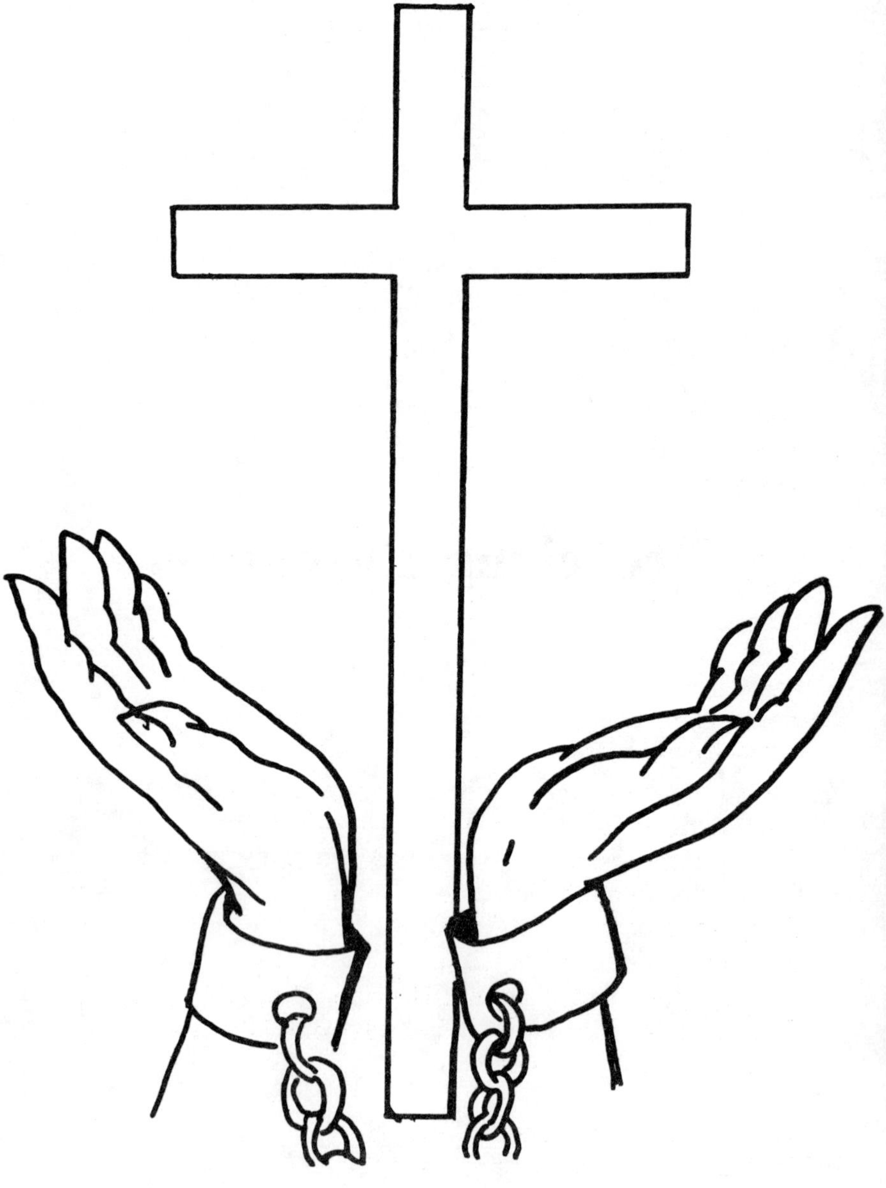

His Hands
James M. Bloom

HIS HANDS . . .
HATH SET ME FREE

"The Spirit of the Lord is upon me, because he hath anointed me to preach the gospel to the poor; he hath sent me to heal the brokenhearted, to preach deliverance to the captives, and recovering of sight to the blind, to set at liberty them that are bruised, to preach the acceptable year of the Lord." (Luke 4:18,19 KJV)

He held in his hands the Word
And the Word became his flesh.
"This day it is fulfilled in your hearing," he said,
This day fulfilled . . . in your hearing.
The elders of Nazareth
Could not believe,
Their eyes blinded to the truth
Of a life full-filled
With God's Spirit.
"Is not this Joseph's son?" they cried.
And their anger rose with wrath
At the impudence of the carpenter's son.
So, raising their hands against him,
They sought to destroy
The blasphemer, Charlatan.
But lay their hands on him they could not.
For he passed through their midst on his way
To do his Father's will.

Jesus held in his hands the tools
To fashion the cradle and yoke
His hands grew strong and hard
As he planed the yielding tree to his will.

Hard was the task of carpenter's hands,
Splintered, bleeding hands,
Bruised by mallet blow.
Hard was the task, but good the trade
Feeding mother and brother and kin.
But answer he must another call.
"Know ye not that I must be about my Father's
business?"

Tender the touch of the Master's hands
Hardened by the labor of younger years.
Gently he lay his hands
Upon the blind to see, the lame to walk.
Setting free the slave,
Healing broken hearts,
Raising the dead
All by the tender touch of hardened hands
Christ preached the gospel to the poor
And God's acceptable year.
But this alone was only part
Of his Father's will.

For word without deed is lost
And heart without hands are waste.
So the touch of his hands
Carried his heart
To do his Father's will.

Mary of Magdala felt his touch.
Seven demons had her soul.
Lust of the eye,
Lust of the flesh
And many more and yet,
When Jesus came
She washed his feet with her tears
And dried them with her hair.
Lovingly, she gave herself
Not for selfish gain,

But a sinner seeking
To love as love should be
Serving the Christ
Who forgave and set her free.
Free to serve in menial task.
Free to kneel in tears before his cross.
Free to stand in joy before his empty tomb.

Blind was he from birth
The man from the city of Siloam.
Some of his friends led him by the hand
To stand before the Lord.
And what did Jesus do?
He spat upon the ground.
Then working between his fingers bold
He fashioned two patches of clay.
And placing his hands upon the sightless eyes,
Gently pressing,
Mostly caressing.
The clay its destined work begun.
Then commanded he,
"Go wash in the pool of Siloam."
And this he did
'Til light, new life
Came sweeping through
And blindness was no more.
For through the touch of the Master's hands
He who was blind, now sees.

When first he heard
His good friend Lazarus
Was dying, almost dead,
He did not hurry to his side
But merely trusted God.
And slowly made his way.
When he arrived
His friend was dead
And kin were sorrowing
"If you'd been here, alive he'd be."

Jesus, placing his hands in theirs,
Wept.
And putting his arms
Around both Mary and Martha
He said,
"He who believes in me lives forever.
Do you believe this?"
And when by graveside still
He commanded the dead to live
And Lazarus came forth.

To heal the broken-hearted
Even to set free from death
So that all might believe
He truly was of God.

Would you be free
From all your sin,
Your cares, your woes,
Your blindness,
Your crippled lives?
He bids us
To surrender whatever binds us.
He will break the fetters
And set us free.
What did it take to make them free,
The things that makes me free.
It took a cross and the Christ thereon
To break the bonds to set me free.
No other way, they say, to make this slave free
Or any other slave.
For we are all slaves to something
And he would have us free.

He is the way
And the life
And the truth that makes us free indeed
For today in your hearing

It is fulfilled.
"The Spirit of the Lord is upon him
To heal our broken hearts,
To deliver us from captivity,
To set us at liberty"
To be the free sons of God.
Able to live in the light and love
Of God's most beloved Son.

‡‡‡‡‡

**HIS HANDS . . .
TOOK A TOWEL**

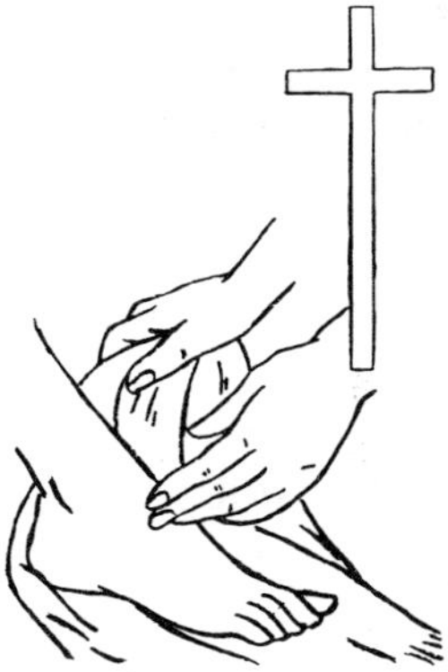

The days bore on
As the Lord drew near
To the fate
That he must face
At the hands of angry men.

Down the dusty roads he went
Down from Galilee,
From the home of his youth,
From Nazareth
To Temple-Town
Where David's throne
Awaits its future King.

Not counting himself an equal with God
For he was; he was,
For he and the Father were one,
He humbled himself
Becoming flesh for us.
He took our human form
Denying the rights of heaven
To be a man for others.
Good news he brought
From heavenly courts

Each child of man is God's
And God still loves
And God still cares
Each child is his own.

Those who cared
And those who dared
Looked in his eyes when he told them.
They couldn't believe their ears.
That the Great God Almighty,
Maker of stars and streams
And the farthest flung creations of the universe
Could love them,
But his eyes were filled with compassion
And they knew the truth of his words.
They knelt in the warmth of his love.
Cleaned through and through.
Though unworthy
His hands touched them
And they felt like new born babes,
Newly wrapped in swaddling clothes
Much as he,
Knowing for a moment
What it must have meant
For God's Own
To be born in a lowly stable.
His hands lifted them up
And he made them stand erect
Proud to be
A part of his Kingdom.

And now
He must be off to Jerusalem
There to finish the job
He came to do.
"The Son of Man must be lifted up
That all men might be drawn toward God."

Many there were
Whose hearts were cold
Not yet pierced by godly fire
Who could not call him Lord.
To call him such
Would disintegrate their power.
So set about they did
To send him to his death.
By trick and betray
They fashioned him a cross.
Knew they not
That this was his aim?
Was it not said of old
Rejected, despised,
Man of sorrows
Would he be?
Bearing in himself
Our transgressions
Our foul and flighty deeds,
Who would have guessed
That the Man of Galilee
Going about doing good
Would come to this ill fate?
But come,
Let us pause
For a meaningful moment
At the threshold of the cross.

It is Passover eve
In an Upper Room
And Jesus
Gathered with the twelve
Partakes of bread and board
Then, knowing that God
Had put all things in his hands,
He rose from supper
Taking a servant's towel.
He took in his hands a towel,

And girding his waist,
He began to wash his disciples' feet.
A simple act, to be sure,
So common every day.
For the dust upon the travelers' feet
By servant hands so cleansed
'Twas what a good host would do.
One by one
They felt his touch
So tender, so sensitive
To their need.
His hands
Completely aware of their task
Moved on to Peter's feet.

"Oh Lord, Oh Lord," he cried
"It is I your servant should be.
Do not wash my feet;
Let me wash yours."
"But Peter," he said,
"Wash your feet I must.
Lest you be no part of me
For serve I must
So was I sent
A servant your Lord must be."
"If that be so,
Not my feet alone, Oh Lord
Not in part but all of me."
"No need for more than feet right now
I set thee an example.
He who serves would Master be
So do and live."

The night was hard
As it drew on
His hands lifting loaf and cup
His covenant with men
Betrayal already nigh

"Lord, is it I, is it I?"
The servant of the Lord goes forth
To pray with sweat of blood
"Thy will, not mine, be done."

Suffering servant of God,
What are you saying to me?
Must I share the grief?
Must I share the pain?
That you bore
On Calvary?
And not only there
But in the hills of Galilee
Where blind and lame reside?
Where hungry, thirsty souls
Cry out, Oh Lord, How long?
Where imprisoned, naked hearts
Are longing to be free?
And must I bend down
In humility
At my brother's feet
That I may be cleansed
As well as he?

"To the least of these you've done to me."
I must, I must
If I desire to be with him
The suffering servant of our God.
Help my hands to take a towel.

‡‡‡‡‡

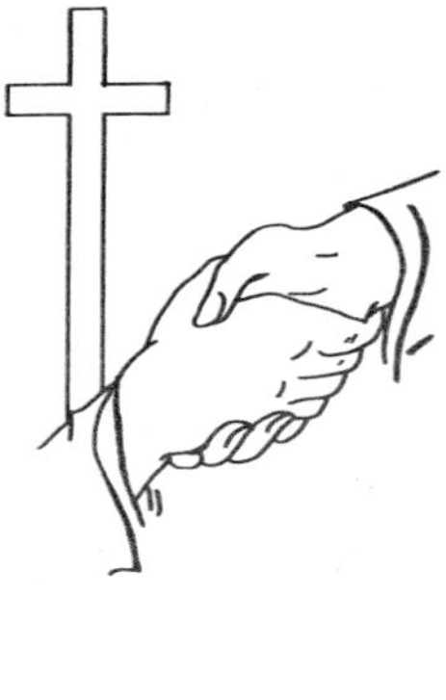

**HIS HANDS . . .
BREAK DOWN WALLS**

In the beginning
God made man for himself,
Out of the dust of the earth

Made he man.
In his own image
Made he man.
Born of God
To live in love
Out of nothingness
He created something
And someone
To live in eternal harmony with him.

But, alas,
Before the dawn of the eighth morning
Man chose
To discard
God's counsel
On getting along in the Garden of Eden.
Man chose
To favor
The pleasure of his own selfish instinct
Which we call sin.
Man began to build a wall
Betwixt himself and God
Even higher
Shutting out
All light
Til groping in the darkness
He cried
"O God, how long
    must I live with my
    self alone, without
    the light of your love?"
Quite often the light broke through
The poorly constructed wall
And with the light
The voice of God
"Here I am
I've always been here,
I will always be here."

"I don't like this wall you've built,
Every time you sin
You wall me out.
Only your cry for my love
Can tumble the wall
That you built.
I will not take it down for you.
But I will always be here
To help you cart it away."
For myriad generations
We have followed
The inclinations of all who went before,
To wall out God
And then to cry for help
When no longer
The light shone through.

A builder of walls is man
To shut out
To shut in
To shelter
To protect
To keep out people we do not like
To keep in all that's precious to our desire.

Walls are built
To separate
Husband and wife,
Father and son,
Neighbors,
Rich and poor,
Black and white,
Protestant and Roman Catholic,
East and West,
North and South,
From each other,
And from God.

There was a wall
Around Jerusalem,
But a gate-crasher
By the name of Jesus
Came riding through.
Upon the foal of an ass came he
Upon the palm-strewn way,
Penetrating deeply
The hearts of Hosanna singers.

Hardened hearts,
With walls of stony glare, shouted
"This man should die
For he breaks down the walls
It has taken centuries to build.
He must die."

Hand in hand
Heart to heart
No matter what one color
Class, or station may be
Sinners all
We may approach God's throne
Brothers, barriers down
That keep us from loving one another.
No longer
Letting pride and self-esteem
Deny
The power of the cross
And the love thereon
To make of many . . . one people
Made in his image
Created to express his love.

Are you willing to share a cross
With one who cuts across
And through
And breaks down all walls,
That God's Kingdom may truly come?

A breaker of walls was he
Breaking down
The walls of hostility
Between God and man
And man and man
Marking and
Crossing for all eternity
The path by which
Men are reconciled to God
And one another.

God never built a wall
He only tolerates them
For a while
Then judgment comes
And mercy strains
And sin receives its wage
A death
A cross
The guiltless one
For all mankind
For all eternity
The perfect sacrifice.

‡‡‡‡‡

**HIS HANDS . . .
REDEEM**

"Thou shalt call his name
Jesus,
For He shall save his people
From their sins."
And Mary
Kept all these things
In her heart.

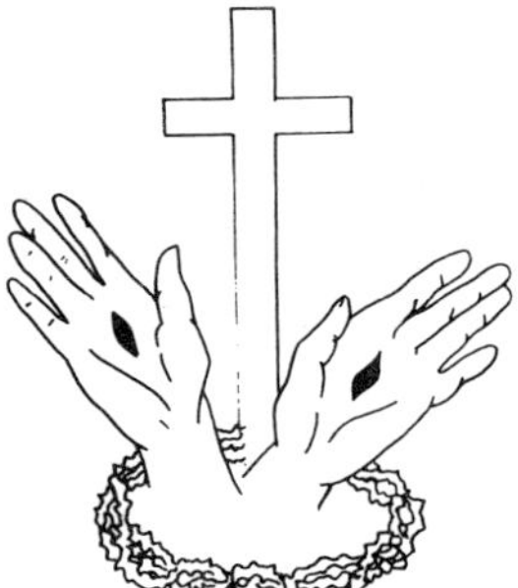

How could a carpenter's son
Save the people of God
From their sins?
Was not the priest
The one to offer sacrifice
For Israel's atonement?
An unblemished lamb
For an altar
A goat sent into the wilderness
To die,
Would not this do
As it had always done?
What more will Jesus do
Than has been done?

Dark was the night
And stark the shadow
Of a cross in their midst
As they dipped their bread
To sup
In a quiet upper room.
All eyes upon him,
He held in his hands the cup,
Thanking God,
Saying,
"My cup,
My blood,
My new covenant,
Running over for you."

A strangeness in his eyes,
Partly sad, yet filled with hope,
Eager to finish his task
To be the perfect lamb
To take away the sin
Of the whole world
For once, for all.

Betrayer, hearken,
Leave the room,
Do what you must do.
The time has come.
The hour is near
Rise up and go.
To the destiny of men who mistake the Master's call.

Dark was the night
Of that human soul
That betrayed my Master and Lord.
Perhaps he thought
A favor he'd do
To force his Master's hand.
Only God knows why
That Christ one step closer might be
To that cross of Calvary
Allowed one of his own to betray.
But the worst of it all
Is he never knew
It was for him as well
That Jesus prayed
"Forgive."
And hanging from a tree
He died the death of remorse.

The others rose
To leave that room
To a garden fair,
One where they had been before.
A place of prayer,
A solace there,
It meant so much to him.

Up the hill went he
And the three beside
To a hallowed, holy place.
"Watch and pray," said he

Knowing the hour of their temptation.
Thrice he prayed and thrice they slept.
Not knowing the agony of his hour.
They slept away
The precious hours
He spent with God
Struggling through the meaning of his hour
And the cross that he must bear.
He held in his hands the cup
As he folded his hands in prayer,
The real cup,
The cup of suffering,
Cup of sorrow.
No other way that he can go.
No other way to redeem.
And placing his hands in God's,
He readied his will to do.

Betrayal at hand,
Soldiers dispatched,
Pharisees and scribes with angry faces
To take the Lord of Lords.
And one who slept instead of praying,
Severed a soldier's ear.

Dark was the night
In Gethsemane
When
Deep in the hearts of men
The evil one possessed
That no man should be free
From its power.
Betrayal,
Greed for power,
Thirst for death,
And fear to stand when all seems lost.

Disciples scattered
"Like a sheep without a shepherd"
And taking my Master's hands
They bound them
And led him away
To die.

They scourged him
And beat him
And made sport of him.
Crown of thorns,
Have you no other place to rest?
Cross of Wood
Have you no other body to bear?
Nails,
Have you no other hands to hold?
This Jesus
Whom you crucify,
Is innocent of blood.
Release him from your hold.

Said the crown, "I cannot pull out my thorns."
Said the cross, "No nail will let loose."
No man saves himself.
He cannot come down.
He came to save others.
"Forgive them
This day."

Great love was on that cross.
A life that dared to love
No matter what the cost.
Hands that hung and bled
Were those
Who blinded eyes had touched,
Broken limbs had healed,
Hands of comfort and assurance,
Hands of peace and anointing,

Hands that calmed the tossed sea,
Hands that loved
And most of all
In that love
Loosed the power of souls
To meet their Maker's goals.

Though all the sins of mankind
Were not found in him
But nailed upon that tree
Our God allowed
Our sins to die there, too.

And we may touch the wounds
Of the hands that bled
That day
And know
By the confession of our lips,
The faith of our heart
That by his grace
And daily strength
To do God's will
That we are redeemed,
No longer bound to sin.
For the Paschal Lamb is slain
For all eternity
And I and the Father are one
As He and the Father are one.

Hallelujah, what a Savior!

‡‡‡‡‡

HIS HANDS . . .
LEAD ME

Of
The lineage of David

Royalty
Dwelt in the Bethany home
Of Mary, Martha, and Lazarus
Unbeknown,
No one
Can fathom the depth of their love
For him.
Knew they not
His cross-laden task?
Anointed One of God,
Appointed Messiah-King
Allowing them to be
His second family.
Martha served him well,
Mary ointment spread upon his tired feet.
Tears of royal hue
Mourned Lazarus, friend and brother.

With hands outstretched
He bid his dead friend rise,
From grave and chains of death
Lazarus broke free.
That they might believe
That truly Jesus was the Christ,
Messiah-King.

From Bethany
From the Mount of Olives
Through Bethphage
To Jerusalem's gate
The good news spread
"The prophet from Nazareth
Raised Lazarus from the grave.

"He draws near to Jerusalem
For the Passover Feast."
No more need be said.
Word became flesh

In the trampling feet
Running to meet
The royal caravan
Of the Galilean seer
And his disciples twelve.
And trailing on behind
Bethany's best.

Standing
On the Mount of Olives
Gave vantage view
Of the city of the King
Rising
To Mt. Zion
Where once David dwelt
Where now Herod's castle gleams.
All the Messianic dreams
Of generations past,
Crumbled neath his gaze.
Did not Jerusalem
Know who they were
To come to this sad state?
God's chosen ones
Had not chosen God.
Even those
Who religion made a slave
Now conspired a prophet's death
As their fathers
Put out the fire that burned
To cleanse
Each man's wayward stance.
"O Jerusalem,
When will you learn
To love as I love you?"
Tears down the cheeks of one who truly loved
Not only a friend, but all mankind.

Down the slope
And across the Kedron Brook
Lay the gate of David's town,
Must stop and pause.
"Go fetch the colt of an ass
Tied to its mother's side.
If anyone asks,
Say the Lord has need of him
And they will let you go."
And it was as he had said.

Brought to him
Some standers-by
Laid their cloaks upon the lowly beast
Too young to know the burden others knew.
Privileged he was
To bear the weight of the one who gave him life.
Ascending upon
The makeshift saddle
His hands took hold the reins
And guided his bearer
Toward Jerusalem.
Lining the way
Were men, women, children
Passover pilgrims
Enthralled
By the prophetic
Entry
Of their predicted King
Riding upon the foal of an ass.

Their hands
Created
By palms and love
A carpet of majestic weave.
Their voices
Rang
In praise and song

"Hosanna, Hosanna
To he that comes,
Hosanna to the Son of David,
Hosanna to the King."

Judas must have been glad,
The other disciples too.
They thought
So this is the way it will be.
Could it be
That Jesus' fears of death
Were false?
The people love him so.
No one dare kill him now
Lest the people rage.
Day of triumph pre-mature,
It seemed so very right.
But only Jesus knew
What suffering he must bear
That King of Kings,
Lord of Lords,
He might be.
Earthly kings
Have their fame,
And gold and property,
Lead the legions of war
To conquer for themselves
And their own
All wealth that can be had.

No one
Knows the suffering
That pains the heart
Of the King who would rule our hearts
And all the hearts of men.
Taking the risk
That we will turn him down
And love another King.

Some would mock his kingly role
As soldiers did that day
"A crown of thorns,
A robe of scorn,
A reed of bitter tree,

The crown cut deep the Kingly brow,
The robe hid much his shame,
The stripes by which we are healed,
His hands held tight the scepter reed
To rule the likes of men
Who knew not what they did."

"Are you a King?"
The Governor cried. "For this end was I born,
Thou sayest it, I am.
My kingdom is not of this world's likes,
It dwells in the midst of men's hearts."

A timid tyrant
Washed his hands
Hoping to rid his heart of this dark stain
Letting the cries
Of a mob
Decide the fate of their real King.
But
One last word would Pilate say
Above the beam
That soon would hold the crucified hands
Outstretched and lifted up toward God.
Jesus, of Nazareth, King of the Jews
In languages three
That all may read and know.

And now I look upon that cross
Knowing full well
That royal blood was shed
Not only David's line,
But God's own Son.

He came,
And lived,
Taught and healed,
Died and rose
That each man
Might invite the King of Love
To rule their hearts and minds.
Who really knows what this world would be
If every man would kneel
Before his cross, his earthly throne
And love as he.
I only know that when I'm his
And he controls
A better man am I.

His hands lead me
Into his Kingdom of Love
His hands hold the sceptre of my life
And nail prints there
And the thorn-crowned brow
Remind me of
The price he paid
To free me from my sin.
Dare I give less
Than all my love
To the wonderful King of Kings.
Desiring to be
Of his royal lineage of love.

‡‡‡‡‡

HIS HANDS . . .
BID ME COME

Tending nets
That day
Along the Galilean Shore
Pre-occupied

By fishermen's task
No notice
We took
Of the stranger
Approaching from afar.
Drawing near
He drew close
As though
He and we stood alone.

He spoke
As if for all our life
He knew us best,
And, taking leave,
He turned
His hands extended
His eyes reflecting
The depth of what must be.
"Come, follow me"
And up we rose
Untangled from the nets
That bound us
To a meaner work
Determined
To do the bidding
Of this Stranger of Galilee.

Others came at his heed
To give their all.
Numbered twelve were they.
Motley crew were we —
Common as the clay
He used to heal the blind man's eyes.

How often he used those hands
To bid come
To all who dare
To serve his Kingdom of Love
How oft.

But a touch
Of my Master's hands
To steal the darkness
From scaled sight
To snatch the demon
Of disease from limb and leg.
To kill the hate
That festered sore heart hearts
Reaching out
To love
Where love has ceased.

"Going fishing"
Was my way
To shove it all aside
But that I could not,
As I thought of his clear call
To be a fisher of men.

And when he rose
He bid me come
With nail-scarred hands
My cross to bear
For him.
To love him sincerely
Feed his sheep
No matter what the cost.

I knew he knew
The price to pay
For all men to be free
A cross, a love that cares,
Denying self
And trusting God.
And each, who
Rising,
Following him,
Must know what it must mean.

A cross I wore
To serve my Lord.

And he bids you come.
Spread your hands
To bid men come
To follow Christ as Lord
And you will find
Your outstretched hands
Nail-scarred
To bear the sin
With Jesus Christ
Of all mankind.
He bids you come.
Are you willing
To be crucified with him
That with him
You may be raised
To eternal life?

Week of weeks
Not forgotten
How he bid us come
Pray with him
An hour.
Sleep was bidding even more
And confident were we
Nothing harmful
Would come near
That Jesus could not stop.

Hurt was he
That we
Whom he had bid come to pray
Could not help
In his darkest hour.
Then and only then
He bid us go

Let free from soldier's grasp
We watched in fright
As bound, his hands no longer free
To bid us come.

He said it would be so
Scattered we would be
And I
So that others might not know
Followed from afar
To see
What they would do
To him who loved me so.
I took the chance
Revealing not my cause
Doing thrice
What I dared not dream.

Hands tied
He bid me with eyes
Gently.
Cleansing me of my sin.
Saying, not yet . . .
Your hour will come.
I saw him on the cross
His hands no longer free
Bound by hammer thrust
To wooden wings.

I could not draw near
To share his mother's grief.
I could not raise my voice
In protest for this deed.
I only grieved
And bled inside
The loss of my Master and Friend.
I had to go
Where first I met

That Stranger
By the shore of Galilee.

‡‡‡‡‡

Sermon Illustrations for Lent and Easter

Old Testament Texts

GENESIS 2:7-9, 3:1-7

After God created the earth, the sun, moon and stars, all forms of vegetation and animal life, then he created man. God breathed into his nostrils and he became a living soul, a living being. Man created in the image of God; the intellectual, moral and spiritual image of God, capable of thinking God's thoughts after him. The following poem illustrates the superiority of man over the animals.

Spiked barbs of remorse
Do not enter the soul of a horse.

The jocund cow
Does not reflect on why and how.

No mention of right and wrong
Is made in the lark's song.

The goat does not waste his time
Considering the concupiscence of crime.

The Peregrin
Has no notion of sin.

Neither does it occur to the mole
To look to the salvation of the soul.

Nothing could be more free
Than the conscience of the chimpanzee.

And every beaver
Is a born unbeliever.

Prayer does not interest a bear.

And not even a dove
Ever got the idea that God is love.
— R. P. Liston, *Atlantic Monthly*, September, 1947

*****

Satan appeared in the form of a serpent and entered into conversation with our first parents. He posed as a friend rather than what he was — an adversary (Satan), as a slanderer (devil). He appealed to the appetite (the tree was good for food). He appealed to avarice (the tree was good to look upon). He appealed to our ambition (you will be like God knowing good and evil). Our first parents yielded to Satan's clever temptations and in so doing they were cast out of the Garden and brought death upon themselves and us.

*****

One of the laws of biblical interpretation is the law of first mention. According to this law the characteristics of a person and his actions when first mentioned will fit the description of that person later on. In the first mention of Satan he is shown to be a liar, deceiver and slanderer and an opponent of both God and man. When Satan tempted our first parents, he appealed to the appetite, avarice and ambition. And Satan used these same methods in the temptation of Jesus in the wilderness. When Jesus was hungry, Satan tempted him to turn the stones into bread and the inference is that Jesus would follow that method in his ministry; i.e., feed the poor and be an Economic Savior. Leaping from the pinnacle of the temple would be an amazing thing and would win Him many followers right at the beginning, so he would be a Sensational Savior. This was an appeal to pride. The third temptation, to gain the kingdoms of the world by worshipping Satan, was an appeal to avarice by which Jesus would be a Warrior Messiah. Jesus knew that was the kind of Messiah the Jews were expecting. So, the temptations of Jesus were real. He was not merely shadow-boxing. Jesus resisted these temptations and angels came and ministered to him.

Then in I John 2:16 the temptations from the world are the lust of the flesh, the lust of the eyes, and the pride of life — the same Satanic methods of appetite, avarice, and ambition.

As in modern warfare, a knowledge of the weapons used by the enemy helps in both defense and offense. So, knowing the weapons the devil uses against us should help us in our struggle against him.

‡‡‡‡‡

GENESIS 12:1-7

These two virtues, faith and obedience, are very closely related. Each one is incomplete without the other. In Abraham's life and work, he illustrates these virtues admirably. When God called him to leave his home where he had lived for 70 years and go out to another land, the land of Canaan, many miles away, "by faith he obeyed." (Genesis 11:9)

And when God told Abraham to offer up his dearly beloved Son, Isaac, as a human sacrifice, that seemed terribly unreasonable, since it would cancel out God's promise that through Isaac a great number of his descendents would come into existence. But "by faith he obeyed." He had enough faith in God's honesty in keeping his promise that God would restore Isaac to life again in case he really had to obey the command of God to slay Isaac and offer him in sacrifice.

These two virtues have characterized God's people down through the centuries. Christ himself set us the example of faith and obedience. He had supreme faith in God, of course, and although he dreaded the crucifixion, in his agony in the Garden, he prayed, "nevertheless, not my will but Thine be done." (Matthew 26:42)

By faith and obedience, Stephen became the first martyr and for the same reason, Peter risked his life when he declared to the Jewish authorities "we must obey God rather than men." And Paul through much persecution and finally martyrdom said, "For me life is Christ, to die is gain." The 11th Chapter of Hebrews reports many who suffered and died for their faith and obedience to God. Since then untold thousands have followed in their train, and in many parts of our world today the persecution of Christians for their faith and obedience is still being carried on.

*****

Abraham and his nephew Lot had prospered in the land of Canaan. They had many flocks and herds and their herdsmen had begun to quarrel among themselves, and the two owners were in danger of becoming involved also. But Abraham said to Lot, "Let there be no strife between us for we are kinsmen." Then very generously he told Lot to make his own choice of the land where he would like to go and find pasture for his cattle and sheep. How greatly is the spirit of peacefulness needed in our world today. Quarreling, fighting, and killing seem to be the order of the day. Within the past two weeks the radio reported three such horrible events right within the families where there should be peace and harmony.

At a thanksgiving dinner an uncle shot and killed his nephew because of a quarrel over who would eat the dark meat of the turkey. In another case a father shot his own son when they quarreled about the son's long hair. In a third instance a man came home and killed his own mother, his wife and three teenage children.

"Be ye kind to one another, forgiving one another, even as God in Christ has forgiven you." (Ephesians 4:31, 32; 5:1)

*****

God greatly rewarded Abraham for his life of service. God fulfilled his promises recorded in Genesis 12:2-3 by making his name great, and making of him a great nation, of blessing him and making him a blessing to all the families of the earth. A blessing to all the families was fulfilled in the life of Jesus our Savior who was in the line of descent. The prophet Isaiah (41:8) quotes God as saying, "Abraham, my friend."

But what about us? We are not Abraham, nor can we fill such an important place as he filled in his life and work. True, but we can all do what is within our reach. Jesus said, "Whatsoever gives a cup of cold water to one of these little ones in my name shall in no wise lose his reward." (Matthew 10:42)

Trust and obey, for there is no other way
To be happy in Jesus, but to trust and obey.

‡‡‡‡‡

GENESIS 22:1-14

The story of stewardship goes back to the beginning of the Bible when, high on a mountaintop, a father actually offered up his little boy. It is the first reliably recorded "pledge" in the Bible.

We moderns, however, have flinched so in horror at this barbaric episode, which God stopped in the nick of time, that we have been afraid to take another look; and we have missed the extraordinary valor and enviable devotion that went, this once, with stewardship. God never meant to let this man make such a mistake, but he could tell easily by that hard test there was no mistake about this man. He was all God's. It was too early in the day of time for Abraham to understand God's methods — how could he know the best way to give a son to God?

But his motive was pure. One has to know the pricelessness of sons in those days, and how many years this old man and woman had waited for a son, to know what this generosity cost. For that father offered God his prize possession, his pride and joy, the apple and the light of his old eyes. And of course God wouldn't take it. But because Abraham did not hold anything back from God, God picked Abraham to play the father to his chosen people and presented him with "children" as the stars in the sky in number.

Giving to God has declined since then. The Sunday morning offering has been slow in sons. We think of small change now — nothing to shake the Dow-Jones averages. We are horrified with Abraham for laying Isaac on the altar. But Abraham would be horrified at the scale of sacrifice we have offered in place of sons. During the Every Member Canvass, God will not have to alert his angels to hold back the hands of his servants for fear they will give too much.

We have lost the lively sense of God's ownership. The sense of belonging to him that Abraham felt has grown stale. Modern eyes have grown unaccustomed to reading God's name on everything.

Dr. Ralph Sockman tells how a New York law firm was engaged to clear title to some property in New Orleans. A New Orleans attorney traced it back as far as 1803, but the New York firm wrote him that he hadn't gone back far enough. In due time they received this letter:

Gentlemen:

Please be advised that in the year 1803 the United States of America acquired the territory of Louisiana from the Republic of France by purchase. The Republic of France in turn acquired title from the Spanish Crown by Conquest; the Spanish Crown having obtained it by the virtue of one Christopher Columbus, a Genoese Sailor, who had been authorized to embark by Isabella, Queen of Spain, who obtained sanction from the Pope, the Vicar of Christ, who is the son and heir of Almighty God, Who made Louisiana.

We have to be reminded "in the beginning God." The recognition of this basic premise is not native. This realization distinguished Abraham from his contemporaries. We have to be taught that "the earth is the Lord's and the fulness thereof." Ordinarily we thank the last person, the one nearest to us, for our benefits. We thank the teacher for junior's improvement; our thanks easily end with the shake of the doctor's hand for our newborn child instead of standing face to face with the Great Physician. We thank the good neighbor for being a good neighbor instead of tracing goodness back and up to him "from whom cometh every good and perfect gift." We have not developed the habit of detecting the hand of heaven in our hour-to-hour affairs. Our imagination has not been stretched this way lately, in office or suburban life, in the last book we laid down or in the first thing we did this morning when we got up.

Man has also lost the consciousness of God in the sense that Abraham, the prophets, and Jesus had it. The idea of God's ever eavesdropping on our conversation or paying any attention to prayers is not very real any more. Religion has shrunk from the electric companionship that Abraham enjoyed to a routine; religion to most men is not a consciousness of God, but a method of thought, a policy. A minister was once asked if the Holy Spirit had ever spoken to him. He thought a minute, then finally volunteered, "Yes, I believe he did once. I heard him just as I was leaving the pulpit. He said, "Klaus, you have been lazy again." At our worst, the visible power of the Holy Spirit is safely frozen in the standard greetings of courtesy given to God correctly in Sunday prayers. The religion that used to walk — take men where they were going — has lain down on the job and is carried now to ceremonies. It is now eccentric for a family to sit down together and consult the will of God before making their decisions.

I think that we have also mislaid not only the sense of belonging and intimacy, but the awareness of personal indebtedness to God. Every Christian knows, when he stops to think about it, that he owes his life and breath and his measure of happiness to his Maker. But it remains for him an academic assent; it is not a stimulating awareness. It does not strike home to him as tangibly as the bills in his morning mail. One detects in Abraham a wrestling with God's Will. There is a pull, a give and take, a responsiveness and responsibility to God that has gone out of the present-day religionist. That is why we will never want to give to God as Abraham did. Today the awful obligation boils down to "What Are Others Doing?"

At a college a few years ago, when a financial campaign was in progress, the chairman of the committee wrote to a famous alumna, "Send us a message for our campaign — and make it gay!"

"Tell them this for me," she wrote back. "Never take your college for granted. A lot of people broke their hearts to give it to you." This calls to mind the greater cost people paid to get Christianity to us — the blood spilled in the Colosseum, the lives lost at sea, the Scripture written in a prison cell.

I don't believe we shall ever know what possessed Abraham to go up the mountain with his boy under his arm — what made Tyndale perish in the flames of the burning stake — what made the illustrious Schweitzer throw away his brilliant career — unless we know a little of what Isaiah meant when he openly discussed God's expenses. The perceptive Isaiah was under the strong impression that in some way God "was wounded for our transgressions," "bruised for our iniquities."

I am sure that if God were to say today, as Isaiah

heard him say: "Whom shall I send, and who will go for us?" that none of us could move a muscle unless we had a moving glimpse of the tearstained face, the crimson back, and mangled hands of a God who has gone through hell for us. It takes that vision to bring a man to his feet to say such a drastic thing as "Here I am! Send me."

All God wants of us is ourselves. He has given us everything, namely himself, and wants us back on our own two feet. Jesus rejected compromising candidates for the Kingdom with strong language. "Foxes have holes, and birds of the air have nests; but the Son of man has nowhere to lay his head." He warned applicants to count the cost. What was it? A Cross.

Christ asks from each of us not just a little spending money, but our lives, our fortunes, and our sacred honor. The vows he requires make those by Arthur's knights feeble by comparison. He is not necessarily asking us to sell everything we have and take to the road. What he is asking from us is a complete reorientation of our lives right where we are. Some of us may have to move; some should do the same things but for different reasons, in a different order, with a different spirit. For many of us the change of direction the New Testament is always talking about should be made at home on our present job — putting his Kingdom first, instead of the reverse. It is a reshuffling, a re-evaluation, doing things in a completely different light. Godliness means we will be beginning and ending our days and our ways in the light of his wishes.

Our money takes our measure in a way that statements from the pulpit or confessions from the pew do not. Our money makes our motives portable. It is transportation, taking us where we wish to go without our having to go there. With money we can go to work in Africa without ever leaving our desk.

We can put the residue of our money aside as spending money for our senior years, or we can use money to buy medicine to free some Indian from his prison of pain. What we do with our money is where our blood, sweat and tears are going. Whatever we do with our money — save it up for descendants, put it into fads or hobbies — the bulk of it goes into whatever our god is. If we have the fortune or misfortune of having a good biographer, he will be more impressed by our checkbook stubs than by our official religious position. Our real religion is where our heart is. It can be a Confucian worship of ancestors and relatives, or a stoic stand on our status quo.

The issue, of course, is deeper than statistics. It is what we put first that really is our first love. In many lives Isaac is not on the altar, not are we fathers on the altar. If we could see past the fog of ecclesistical fuss, we might be shocked to see God himself being sacrificed. What do you and I put first? What dictates our stewardship policy? Is it safety first, social approval, a bribe to make God forget where our heart is? These are the deep waters of God's judgment and each man's most important business.

But this must not divert us from the practical matter of making a pledge. The brass-tacks question today and every day — for the few days we have left in life — is "Who will be my God?" And "What shall I give him?"

We all resent men's manufactured exploitation of our obligation to God. We don't have to walk down the sawdust trail just when the evangelist says so in order to prove we're Christian. Every man can make his gift to God in his own way in his own good time. That is between him and God. The Every Member Canvass should be a help, but it is not intended to be pressure. Anyone who knows anything about our operation knows that, if anything, the Church is altogether too timid about money.

But the question remains: "What will I give to God for the whole next year?" His busness cannot run on the piggy banks of camp followers. It stands or falls on the stewardship of the people, not the surplus of the people.

We pick out our gifts for friends very carefully. We certainly will not give them the same things this year we gave last year. Unavoidably the value of our gift conveys the extent of our affection. God can't help drawing conclusions if our Christmas-shopping bill exceeds his gift.

Shall our gift be a sop or a sacrifice? A son? Abraham was ready to give God what he wanted. What does God want you and me to give? This is the time of the year, the time in our lives, to think bravely about these things — and to remember also that when Abraham obeyed God, he was not impoverished but blessed beyond his wildest dreams.

‡‡‡‡‡

EXODUS 33:12-23

YET THOU HAST SAID, 'I KNOW YOU BY NAME.'

How often in Holy Scripture the promise of personhood is carried out by Almighty God. As for instance, when he speaks through Isaiah in the first verse of the 34th Chapter: *"Fear not, for I have redeemed you. I have called you by name, and you are mine."* Or as that promise is fulfilled in the New Testament in John 10:3: *"He calleth his own sheep by name."* Think of the wonder of it that the individual human being is known to Almighty God by name. The deepest desire in the heart of every person is to have this individuality, not only before God, but in the presence of society, and one of the real tragedies of present society is the destruction, progressively, of our personhood. Ours is a time when we have learned to make machines so much like man in their behaviour that they seem almost human. They calculate, they respond, they make decisions, they run factories and pilot airplanes, but another much more subtle and insidious fact of our day is eveident that humans are beginning to act like machines.

We are becoming depersonalized. The very real, alarming and devastating specter of a kind of spiritual leukemia is before us, the inner destruction of man as man, as a person.

Look at the symptoms close at hand in our daily lives. Our lives are speeded up, and the very speed itself serves to depersonalize us. The person in the car in the next traffic lane on the freeway becomes to us just another wheeled adversary. The pedestrian in the crosswalk becomes nothing more than a frustrating pause on the road. Our relations with our neighbors and even our families become fleeting and impersonal. Soon people become things to us, the "thou" becomes an "it," a cashier becomes a hand with money, the waitress becomes a tray with food, a clerk becomes a voice with answers, a wife a cook with sex, a parent, in the eyes of a child, just a disturbing break in the daily television routine. Soon we measure the value of a person in terms of what he can get or give. We become, as Erich Fromm terms us, "marketing personalities," what David Reisman speaks of as "the other directed lonely crowd," what William White has called "the organization man — more organization than man."

*****

I remember the most devastating thing about job hunting as a high school graduate in the midst of the Great Depression was the monotonous regularity with which I was told by a prospective employer: "I can't use you." Have we ever thought what a horrible things that is to say to another human being? I can't use you! Obviously, unless I could be used, I was of no value to anyone. So, individually, we feel lost, lonely, separated and unloved.

*****

If we look at the Church, the institution which ought to be devoting itself to the growth and development of persons, what do we find? Quota madness, statistics, forms, committees, pastors so well organized that they have no time for persons. We no longer have sanctuaries, we now have plants, mimicking the assembly line sterility of the modern corporation. We have staffs, mirroring the bass of the military echelons. Of course, we make organized efforts to redeem the situation. We aren't totally unreflective about it. A typical solution? An official greeter or a greeting committee, the appointed persons-for-the-day. They meet you at the door as you enter the Church. They give you a cursory greeting, a bulletin, a smile and a seat, and this will make you feel wanted. In a very real sense, the bearded and sandaled hippie is a more prophetic instrument of God than many in the Church. He is saying, if we can hear what he is saying: "I'm human. Only so far will you organize and conform my life. You will treat me as a person, or you will not treat me at all."

*****

The story *Up the Down Staircase* is a story of a teacher who takes as her first teaching assignment a class in the ghetto of New York City in a high school. The story tells of her difficulties relating to this mixed racial class of deprived children. Finally, she puts a small question box on her desk, and she tells the children that anything they want to say to her, they can write on a slip of paper and put in the box. This fails to elicit any response, until she finally receives a small slip of paper in the box. She finds out later that it had been written by a Puerto Rican boy who, when he was in school at all, would sit back in the corner of the room, antagonistic, uncooperative, completely at odds with the teacher. Plaintively he had written on the little slip of paper: "I wish you knew who I was." Here is the cry that comes out of our crowded ghettos everywhere: "I wish you knew who I was," — the cry for recognition of our individuality and our personhood.

*****

Norman Cousins puts it this way: "Impersonality is epedemic. It is almost as though we feared contact, almost as though the soul of man had become septic. If a man becomes ill, he hardly hangs up his hat in the doctor's office before he is placed before a whole battery of machines and testing devices. The traveled road is not between the mind of the diagnostician and the heart of the patient, but between the clinic and the laboratory. If a man submits himself for a job, he is seen, not as a personality, but as a fit subject for various tests which presumably have more to do with ascertaining his worth than the human responses which may figure largely in the work that he is called on to do.

Morris Bishop has caught the spirit of our day in the lines he calls *The Perforated Spirit:*

"The fellows up in personnel
Have a set of cards on me.
The sprinkled perforations tell
My individuality.

And what am I? I am a chart
On the cards of I.B.M.
The secret places of the heart
Have little secrecy for them.

It matters not how much I prate
They punch with punishment the scroll
The files are masters of my fate
They are the captains of my soul.

Monday my brain began to buzz
I was in agony all night
I found out what the trouble was —
They had my paper clip too tight.

‡‡‡‡‡

NUMBERS 21:4-9

"And the people spoke against God." [*Numbers 21:5*] Students do that now as much as the mob that dragged its feet behind Moses.

Chaplain Ernest Gordon of Princeton University reports a hospital call he made on a senior just as he was emerging from the anesthesia. He let God have it with no holds barred.

I know who you are. I'm not surprised you are here. For some reason, I thought of you. When you came into the ward, I was thinking what a damn funny thing it was to do that. It's this God stuff, that's what it is. I must have been scared into thinking of him. But I'm not going to be fooled. I know why you turned to him. It was because you were chicken, that's what you were. You couldn't face this fouled-up crap-ridden world, so you ran to him. Not me! You won't catch me doing anything so stupid. I know what it's all about.

You do? You've been assuming that I don't. Tell me.

It's about nothing. That's what it is. Just a big fat, juicy, dripping hole. If there's a god, that's what he is.

That doesn't leave very much, does it? Why, then, are you so darned angry? Why get angry about nothing?

Because everything is so rotten. God, what a world! The only thing that I can do is to hate him for starting it.

Well, that is something. It is better than nothing. Maybe you can only hate him because you're afraid to love him?

That's the screwed-up sort of thing I might have expected you to say. You're trying to fool me into believing that things are better than they are. You are a hope merchant. That's what you are selling. You're trying to believe that this dung heap of a world will get better, or that the good will be given an acre in heaven when they die. But I know better. Things will get worse. The politicans will screw us. The poor will get poorer. We'll get rid of those we don't want by having a war for the sake of peace. Then we'll all blow up. The last big bang will be the best bang of all. That's where your hope will take us.

You can't get away with murder of God like that. *"Then the Lord sent fiery serpents among the people, and they bit the people so that many people of Israel died."* [*Numbers 21:6*] While a man must be honest to God in his hate, and that frank hatred is far superior to pretended love, no one can continue to stand up against God without getting hurt. Attacking God still acts upon a man like snakebite. A man filled with hate against God is filled with poison. Anyone who cannot or does not stop is in hell. A man who shakes his fist and grinds his teeth against God is a dead man. He has bitten the hand that feeds him. Someone may break himself breaking any of the commandments, but breaking the first commandment is dead wrong.

Nicky Cruz was filled with hate. He fed on hate. He forged his gang with hate. The venom would have killed him had it not been lanced by the love of Christ. Faced with this love in the flesh the hate drained from him. He remembered when it first entered. A neighbor told his mother that she looked like little Nicky. The mother made no comment. That confirmed Nicky's mounting suspicion. She did not love him. He went to bed ravaged with a hate that had him in its strangling power until a higher power undid it by his loving life and death.

When the people of Israel realized that they were dying from the venom they repented. *"So Moses made a bronze serpent, and set it on a pole, and if a serpent bit any man, he would look at the bronze serpent and live."*

[*Numbers 21:9*]

‡‡‡‡‡

DEUTERONOMY 26:5-10

One of the main thrusts that I see in this lesson is the call to the Christian to continually renew (remember) his vertical relationship to God, a relationship that is, by its nature, deeply rooted in the Judaeo-Christian tradition and the whole history of salvation. We need to remember that we are not simply "now" people, but are, basically, a continuing part of a history that is founded in and rooted in a vertical relationship to God who chose us. Hence, that entire history from Creation on down through the Old and New Testaments and the history of the Church is a part of our "now" story. That whole history looks down upon us, as it were, and we are called to remember it and to be alert to the past from which we were hewn.

An illustration that points to this idea involves Napoleon. He is reputed to have been one of the world's champion leaders of men. He could, it is said, inspire people as few men have been able to do throughout history. By this gift, Napoleon rose from a general in the French Republican Army to Emperor of a vast kingdom. He is attributed with saying, to his tired, worn soldiers whose morale was pitifully low, during his campaign to win Egypt, "From yonder pyraminds, forty centuries are looking down on you." And with that, he helped his men gain a sense of the movement of history. He told them that they were a part of the gigantic, momentous movement of history — so on to victory. Countless centuries look down upon contemporary Christians and we are part of that even more gigantic momentous history, the history of salvation and God's dealings with us.

*****

Another example of the great importance of keeping remembrance of our tradition always before us is seen in the quite common problem of the vertical adjustment on the television screen. When it goes awry, the total experience of involvement in the program is ruined. Both the vertical and the horizontal must be tuned in properly if the viewer is to know what's going on in his picture tube. Christians need the continual reminder that discipleship, obedience, mission *now* must be rooted in all that *has been*, for we are a part of that continuing history.

*****

As we are called to remembrance and dedication, we are called to remember *the* basic: Christ died on the cross to forgive us our sin. We are also called to dedicate ourselves anew to living in the love which forgiveness grants us. The following true story is somewhat emotional, but then most of the confrontations I have experienced between God and any person have involved feelings as well as intellect.

A. Leonard Griffith, several years ago as pastor of the City Temple in London, wrote: "An Archbishop of Paris was preaching to a great congregation in Notre Dame. He told the story of three young men, gay* and worldly and godless, who wandered into the cathedral one day. Two of them wagered the third that he would not make a bogus confession. He accepted the wager. The priest, who listened, realized what was happening, so when the pretending penitent had finished, he said, 'To every confession there is a penance. You see that great crucifix over there? Go to it, kneel down, and repeat three times as you look up into the face of the Crucified, 'All this you did for me, and I don't care a

*I wanted to keep the quote intact, but "gay" obviously has meanings today not intended by Mr. Griffith.

damn!' The young man emerged from the confessional box to report what had happened and to claim the wager from his companions. 'Oh, no,' they said, 'first complete the penance, and then we will pay the wager.' Walking slowly to the great Crucifix, he knelt down and looked up into that face with its searching eyes of aggrieved love. Then he began, 'All this you did for me, and I . . .' He got no further. Tears flooded his eyes. His heart was torn by the pain of repentance. There his old life ended, and there the new began. Finishing the sermon, the Archbishop said, 'I was that young man.' "

The contemporary Christian, called to a confrontation to remember Christ's action in his behalf, is called to the penance of facing the Crucified as that young man was called.

‡‡‡‡‡

ISAIAH 12:1-6

A sermon about God's triumphant grace could reaffirm the Christian belief that his grace does, indeed, always triumph. People who can recall the anguish following World War II, as well as during it, and people who can by experience or imagination sense what it would be like to be a dominated people, may gain some reassurance from the words of the late Bishop Otto Dibelius as he spoke about the German people under foreign rulers: "God has not yet spoken his last word, and his last word is never judgment but grace . . . I know that God's last word will be a word of grace. That lets us go joyfully into each new day that God gives us . . . Therefore, we dare not be pessimists. Neither dare we be skeptics. We remain God's rejoicing people and look ahead, up, and out of this present valley."

*****

The following story could be used as a basis to point

out some of the plights we need to be delivered from. I have put in italics the points from this fable which relate to some of the things we pursue diligently, frantically in our day.

In one story of the Holy Grail, a knight rode forth in searth of *fulfillment.* He came to a singing brook, deep meadows, trees plentiful with fruit. But even as he ate the fruit, it turned to dust. No *feeding of the flesh* could satisfy his deepest hunger.

Further on he saw a home, a lovely woman standing in its open door, her eyes innocent and kind and all her bearing gracious, and he thought that surely the *love of a woman and the shelter of a home* would be his answer; but she, too, fell into dust at his touch and the home crumbled into a broken shed.

Later in his journey, the knight came to a warrior clad in golden armor; but the warrior, too, turned into dust, for the deepest meaning of life is not in the *pride of battle.* And still later he saw a city on the hill, at its gates a great throng shouting his praises as he climbed the slope, so that he felt that surely *civic honor and the esteem of others* would be his deepest need, but the city and its people were gone when he reached the crest of the hill. So he cried out, in Tennyson's words, "Lo, if I find the Holy Grail itself and touch it, it will crumble into dust!"

A concluding point could be made that God's triumphant grace offers us deliverance from the disappointments that always follow when we look for salvation in the contemporary equivalents of the points made above, as surely we do.

*****

At this writing, just a few days before Christmas, merchants across the country are confidently predicting an average eight to ten percent increase in seasonal sales — over last year's dramatic increase of twenty-six percent! Despite that fact, note that we now face an uncertain economy: that some predict recession, in varying degrees; that layoffs in many an industry have already been made or announced. The juxtaposition of these facts says something of the plight from which we need to be delivered: our seeking fulfillment in things and our hope that, when we give things, we will help someone else fulfill himself.

*****

In considering a sermon on God's triumphant grace, let's not forget the obvious — we are marching through Lent, a time of repentance in which we've been considering sin and suffering and man's plight. But our sights are set on the triumph of Lent when the cross that seemed the ultimate defeat was dramatically turned into God's ultimate triumph! As on the First Sunday in Lent, a simple proclamation of this is in order so that God's people will renew their vertical relationship and dedicate themselves anew in gratitude.

‡‡‡‡‡

ISAIAH 42:14-21

1. God destroys as well as preserves [*Isaiah 42:14*]

Luther says that God is to be both loved and feared. The same God of compassion who is eager to show love to those who turn to him is equally determined to root out and destroy evil. Isaiah is warning us not to be lulled to sleep by thinking only of the kindness of God. He who shows patience toward our waywardness will eventually cease to overlook unatoned sin and will destroy. He holds all the power of the universe in his hands to work his ends. Our eternal destiny is for him to determine. Are we tempting God by clinging to things he opposes? Remember God has said, "I will destroy." The time to repent and make peace with him is now.

2. Christ will restore sight [*Isaiah 42:16*]

A blind beggar walking down a street on a day in spring carried a sign saying, "It is April, and I am blind." How pitiful that he was blind at any time. But on a spring day it was even worse; he could not see the newly formed leaves on the trees, or the beautiful flowers blooming on every hand. He could not see the earth bathed in sunshine or the glow of a sunset in the western sky. But another blindness is even worse. It can come to those who have retained their physical sight. There is a saying, "None is so blind as he that will not see." When Isaiah talks of the blind he includes everyone who does not have spiritual insight. Children laugh at the phrase, "I see, said the blind man." Yet it is true that the physically blind can see many things which the person with sight overlooks. So God promises to help us in our spiritual blindness. He will show us the path of righteousness, reveal opportunities to serve our fellow man, to improve ourselves, and to see the Christ who is hidden from those who do not believe in Him.

3. Idolators shall be ashamed [*Isaiah 42:17*]

Idol worship seems like something out of the long past. It brings to mind visions of ignorant people in an earlier age bowing down before a statue which to them is their god. So this verse does not seem to apply to the one who reads it today. Here is where we deceive ourselves. Idolatry is a very subtle thing. It was said of Sampson that he did not know when the Lord had forsaken him, and thought he could go on in strength as he had before. So idolatry creeps upon anyone who is not alert. It is so easy to cater to oneself; to want fame and fortune so badly that we slowly let these desires come between us and God. Beware lest great shame come upon you because idols of today have subtly replaced God in your objectives and desires.

4. God will be praised for his law (Gospel) [*Isaiah 42:21*]

Our age is one of much disdain for God's law. The ten commandments are regarded by many as out of date. They are as foolish in disdaining God's rules and thinking they have outgrown them as was a certain sailor. The captain had pointed out the north star before turning over the wheel to the young seaman. He told the young man to steer constantly toward that star. The captain then took a nap and upon awakening found that the ship was not on course. When he questioned the young sailor what had gone wrong, he was told, "I have sailed past that star, show me another one." No one can sail past the ten commandments. They remain as up-to-date as the day's news announcements. God has chosen to give honor to his eternal rules, whether they be revealed in the Ten Commandments or in Jesus Christ. The wise will realize the worth of God's laws and strive to obey and honor them.

‡‡‡‡‡

ISAIAH 43:16-21

This message to the Hebrews in exile suggests a gospel proclamation to us in exile today. Although ours is not geographical or, generally, physical, it is spiritual and it is relational. The loneliness of a great number of humans in 1977 is a horror to them. Witness: most of us are never alone without a radio or TV going. We tend to feel that, if we have something around us, we can forget that inner exile that separates us from sensing that life is meaningful and that we are meaningful.

Because there is a similarity in this theme with other lessons of this season, it occurs to me that a sermon on this text could well be one which appeals primarily to emotions — a proclamation that would buoy up the spirit of the hearer and renew his confidence in the God who promises not to abandon his people but, because he once delivered them, to deliver them again.

*****

This might be another good time to call to the people's memory again what God did on the Cross. The incarnation-crucifixion-resurrection could be parabled in this story.

A man was taking a walk through a pasture. He came upon an anthill and amused himself by watching the ants as they busily scurried in and out. Then he happened to move into a position which cast his shadow over the anthill. Immediately all activity ceased. The ants disappeared into their home. When he stepped back so that his shadow was not over the anthill, the ants resumed their activities.

Intrigued by the ants' reaction to shadow and light, he proceeded to conduct a little experiment. He repeated his movements and noticed that each time his shadow crossed the anthill, all activity stopped. Evidently they were afraid of the sudden darkness, he concluded. He wondered how he could prove to the ants that he meant them no harm. He concluded, finally, that the only way he could do this successfully would be to become an ant himself. Then he could communicate with the ants; he could convince them that he wanted to be their friend.

The spiritual and relational exile that we find around and within us so much today could be compared to a darkness — a loneliness in which we fear harm or, worse, meaninglessness. God cut through that darkness in his Son — by becoming human and communicating with us. He went further than the man in the story, though; He died to give us a relationship which would be meaningful and which would eradicate our alienation and loneliness.

*****

We need to be reminded today that Christ is alive! Martin Niemoeller, after World War II, remarked, "The one thing that Adolf Hitler forgot was that Jesus Christ is alive." That is a ringing assurance for us in the tribulations that have our world whirling.

*****

God's promise not to abandon those whom he chooses, in the darkness analogy, suggests that in the night of our exile we can be confident that God will bring daylight again!

The well-known Snoopy, from *Peanuts*, was perched atop his dog house in the dark of the night. His thoughts and fears almost did him in: "Everything seems so hopeless at night. What am I doing here? What's the purpose of it all? . . . What if I get sick? I don't want to get sick . . . What if I get hit by a car someday and end up in a body cast? Or maybe they'd just shoot me like an old farm horse!" By daybreak Snoopy falls asleep. In the later morning sunlight, Lucy and Linus walk by and Lucy comments on the apparently sleeping dog: "It must be nice to be a dog. They don't ever have any worries." And Snoopy the hound thinks happily, "Not as long as the sun is up."

Reminded that God once shone a brilliant light into the night sky and then turned a Friday's darkness into Easter's sunlight, we can have the feeling of confidence that God will turn the darkness of our exile to sunlight once again.

‡‡‡‡‡

ISAIAH 50:4-9a

1. The proper use of wisdom [*Isaiah 56:4*]

Here we are told that the Lord gives us wisdom to be able to encourage the weary people of the world. The

Scriptures declare elsewhere that "the fear of the Lord is the beginning of wisdom." In both instances wisdom and God are tied together. Knowledge can be self-serving, but wisdom leads us in the way of God. This is the day of many counsellors. Psychiatrists, psychologists, ministers, school counsellors are beseiged with calls for help. The Christian has a special opportunity to counsel by passing along the wisdom which comes from the Lord and a knowledge of the Bible. God has made us wise unto salvation not just to harbor that wisdom unto ourselves. "Ye shall be my witnesses," said Christ. Like Isaiah, if we are true to our calling, we shall pass on the wisdom God reveals to us, to help his weary ones. Ours is the word of hope and good cheer; even death has been overcome. Ours is the word of friendship, the word of inspiration. Are we giving it to God's weary ones?

2. God removes dismay [*Isaiah 50:7*]

Note that Isaiah says "Because the Lord God helps me I will not be dismayed." People try to find encouragement and security in many things, mostly material, but God is the one trustworthy source for help in the midst of troubles. During the war when a city was badly bombed a home was demolished. Perishing in the destruction were a mother and her daughter. As the father and his little son probed among the ruins the father was horribly grief-stricken and believed that for him this was the end of everything. Suddenly he missed his small son and when he found him nearby he asked what he had been doing. The lad replied, "I have been watching God hang out the stars." When the outlook is not good, try the uplook. This is sage advice. God is the source of help in every time of trouble.

‡‡‡‡‡

ISAIAH 55:1-7

"WHY DO YOU SPEND. . . YOUR LABOR FOR THAT WHICH DOES NOT SATISFY?"

A woman in our parish referred a lady to me for consultation, and the parishioner said of her friend: "I don't know what her problem is. She has a very successful husband. She is certainly a success at everything she tries herself. I really can't understand what her difficulty is." But when the lady came in, she placed her finger precisely on her problem, as she said to me: "You know, it seems that nothing I do feels important." You see, she was identifying her problem. She said: "I try to do things, and I'm successful at them, but somehow, I always end up by asking myself, 'What's the use?' " Her self-diagnosis was correct. She had identified not only her problem, but the pressing problem of our day. Success in life is not our chief concern. Actually, when you get down to cases, it's not very difficult to be a success in our society today. With average intelligence and a bit of honest application, we can be a success in almost any reasonable type of enterprise. Her problem and ours is not success but significance. It's a rather tragic and sobering fact that according to surveys about seventy-five percent of the people in our nation are working at jobs that they don't really like. Three out of four housewives don't like housework. Three out of four laborers don't like laboring. Stenographers don't like stenography, and even many executives wish that they were doing something other than what they are. Art Linkletter was interviewing a little boy on his program, and he asked the six year old what he wanted to be when he grew up, and he said: "I want to be a fireman." "Why do you want to be a fireman?" "Because my father says I'm just dumb enough to be one." "Oh, what does your father do?" "He's a fireman." And so it is we look at these tasks, and we ask: "What's the use?" For us, there is no significance.

*****

A hundred years ago the average factory worker worked about seventy hours each week, and machines did about six percent of the work. Today he works forty hours or less, and machines do eighty-five percent of the work. But, obviously, that hasn't solved the problem. It hasn't given any more meaning or significance to his task. For most, it is still drudgery. Our problem as we have said, is to have meaning, a significance in life, in whatever system we live, in whatever tasks we are engaged. Even the pagan philosopher, Aristotle, 2,000 years ago said that happiness comes from some productive act, a working in the way of excellence. He was keen enough to see that not even in his primitive, and what we would term barbarian, civilization, our happiest moments are not those in which we ask ourselves to be happy, but rather those in which we lose ourselves in some creative task that seems important. We become so engrossed in that that we forget to take our own emotional pulse. People who have not found joy in productivity must constantly be striving for some pleasure in life, be it play or alcohol, sex or some other sensuous experience, and thus, ironically and paradoxically, the pleasure becomes the index of their unhappiness. Watch a person who is always looking for some kind of pleasure or recreation, and you are looking at a person who is unhappy.

*****

I remember one time I was walking along Times Square in New York, and I passed a little bar that had a sign hanging outside which read: "Come on in. There is never any dull lull in here." Well, that was quite a claim. I thought I ought to investigate, so I went in. What did I see? A picture of human happiness? The customers were sitting along on the bar stools staring at themselves in the bar mirror with obvious distaste. The bartenders were looking back at them with the same expression. If that wasn't a dull lull, then I don't know what a dull lull is. I wonder sometimes with the millions of bar stools in the country whether anyone has ever found happiness on one of them. Our problem is to take life seriously, to be able to believe the primary fact that our lives have meaning and purpose, that there is a reason for living.

*****

Father John Powell has said: "God does not create in order to acquire something, but in order to give something, to share Himself, in other words, to love. And God, whose very nature is love is, obviously, the model of our love." The crusty old sports announcer, Red Barber, once said: "When I boil down thirty years of experience in interviewing people on the radio and TV and put it into one word, I would have to say that the Greeks have a word for it, 'agape.' " Agape means, broadly, "to have concern for." To use Michener's phrase: "There is no real coming home to oneself until our goals and our motives are rooted in unselfish love in agape. This is our reason for being. This is our reason for doing. This is our reason for living."

The newspaper carried the story of a man who had bought himself a new Cadillac. He noticed as he was driving the Cadillac that every time he would hit a slight bump or something, there was an awful thumping in the car someplace. Several times he took it in to be examined and serviced, but they never could find the cause, but always there was this thumping. Finally, he narrowed it down to one door of the car, and they took that door apart. Inside they found a coke bottle, and in the bottle was a note which read: "So you finally found me, you wealthy bastard." You see, the worker wasn't destroying the owner's satisfaction like he thought he was. He was destroying his own, because he wasn't performing his task in love for the man who would someday own the car that he was helping build. Psychologist Murray Banks tells us that old age, if you want to talk about old age, physically, really sets in about the age twenty-eight, because that's when the body begins to disintegrate and deteriorate. But creative love, and real life surge of productivity, is not fully developed until we are about forty. For instance, artists do their best work at the age of fifty or over. Surgeons do their best work at fifty-four. Attorneys are best equipped at fifty-seven to be the most productive and of the greatest service. And yet, at this age, many men are considering retirement.

‡‡‡‡‡

DANIEL 3:8-25

"BUT I SEE FOUR MEN LOOSE . . . AND THE APPEARANCE OF THE FOURTH IS LIKE A SON OF THE GODS."

It was my privilege to appear on the same television program with Julie Bengston, the Heart Sunday Queen of the Heart Association of the State of Iowa. Julie is ten years old. In the course of her young life, she has had six open-chest surgical operation. She is on the fourth pacemaker placed in her body to keep her heart running regularly. Her parents spoke to me and both assured me that it was the miracle of the grace of God that she was still living, a happy, intelligent, well-adjusted child. Her mother told me that for safety's sake, she drove her to and from school, but the little girl decided that she would like to walk home from school alone. Her mother was very fearful to allow her to do this, and she said: "But Julie, if something should happen to you and you should fall down, you would just lie there alone." Julie objected to that. She said: "Why, Mother, if something happened to me and I fell down, I would not be alone. Jesus would be there." A little child shall lead them.

*****

Back in 1917 during the Russian Revolution, a Russian Orthodox priest and eleven of his parishioners were placed in a prison by the Bolsheviks. They were left there to rot. From time to time, as the weeks went by, the guard of the prisoners would tell his superior: "There is someone else in that cell besides those twelve men. There is someone getting to them who helps them and provides them with what they need. I don't know how this is possible. All I know there has to be someone with them." Finally, the superior of the prison impatiently went to the cell with the guard. They opened the cell door and herded the twelve prisoners out into the corridor. The superior counted them off one by one. He said to the guard: "Now, you see, there are only twelve." But the old priest spoke up: "But you have forgotten to count the thirteenth who has always been with us. You have forgotten to count Jesus Christ."

*****

Again and again, in the fires of life, we have seen people standing unharmed and unafraid, because the Lord is with them. Emily Bronte, the author of *Wuthering Heights*, lived and wrote in a rectory on a bleak, gray moor in Yorkshire. She spent her days with a half demented father, two sisters who were dying of tuberculosis, and a brother who regularly came home howling drunk from the village tavern. Yet she could write:

No coward's soul is mine,
No trembler in the world's storm-troubled sphere,
I see heaven's glory shine,
Faith shines equal, arming me from fear.

Jesus walks our lonesome road. He knew heartaches and tears. He knew rejection and ostracism. He knew the loneliness that comes from standing alone for a great cause. He knew defeat and fatigue. He understood life as we face it. He knew the answers. He found that he had company on the lonesome road. He found the Father with him. He spoke those comforting words from which every lonely person can take heart: "I am not alone, because the Father is with me." I love that scene in *Green Pastures* when the children of Israel have gone on ahead into the Promised Land, and they have left Moses behind on Mount Pisgah on the other side of Jordan. What a pitifully lonely figure he is, as he watches them go, and what a terrible lonesomeness descends upon him. Then he hears a movement behind him, and he feels a hand on his shoulder. He asks: "Is you with me, Lord?" The voice that comes back warms his soul: "Cou'se I is, Moses, cou'se I is."

‡‡‡‡‡

ZECHARIAH 9:9-12

"LO YOUR KING COMES TO YOU. TRIUMPHANT AND VICTORIOUS IS HE, HUMBLE AND RIDING ON AN ASS, ON A COLT, THE FOAL OF AN ASS."

Surely one sign of the lack of perceptiveness of us humans is sometimes we don't know when we are being ridiculed, laughed at, satirized, made fun of. I remember when we arrived in Japan for the occupation years ago, the missionary's son who was our regimental interpreter, told me to watch how the Japanese people greeted me. If they would bow and say "Koneechiwa Gozaimas" they were indicating that I was a very honorable person. If they bowed twice, they were indicating that I was a very, very honorable person, but if they bowed three times, they were making fun of me. They were indicating that I thought that I was more honorable than I really was. This is one of the great thrusts of Holy Scripture that we fail to recognize. We don't see when Almighty God is making fun of us. We can't seem to understand when God is laughing at us. The Word warns us: *"He who sits in the Heavens shall laugh. He shall hold you in derision."* But when it happens, we don't catch it at all. We don't get it. We don't understand the satire.

*****

Why do you think God allowed his only-begotten Son to be born in a livery stable? Why was he born in a one-horse town that was the least of Judah? Oh, yes, He was born the Son of a son of David, but that son was only a carpenter, and he certainly wasn't on any social register. Why do you think that his disciples were all peasants? Why did Jesus pal around with the cheating tax gatherers and with the other outcasts of the society? Why did he walk through hated Samaria and associate with people from that half-breed, heretical race? And now why, again, this Palm Sunday procession?

Oh, don't you see? God is laughing at us. He is satirizing our own behavior. "Triumphal entry" you call it? Nothing could be further from the truth. Could anything be more stupid and clumsy looking than an unbroken ass' colt? The sophisticated people of Jerusalem looked down their aristocratic noses from the cool shadows of their balconies to see what all the shouting was about, and all they saw was a motley mob of hicks from the sticks waving palm branches and the very clothes off their own backs. Quite a show! Just about as exciting as a couple of dozen hippies engaged in a march on Washington, and I'm sure that it caused just about the same amount of stir in the City of Jerusalem.

*****

Never did a story build up to a bigger letdown. The palm wavers obviously thought that Christ was riding in to take over the government of the Jews. The Kingdom had come at last! And here they were right in the front pew! They watched him as he stopped the procession and went into the Temple, and when he was inside, they waited breathlessly for some cataclysmic sign from Heaven. And what happened? Nothing! Absolutely nothing! In fact, even the Gospel writers couldn't quite get the flat taste of it out of their mouths. Mark ends his account by saying: *"He went into the Temple, and when He'd looked around at everything, the hour already being late, He went out again."* Period! That's it!

Don't you see, beloved, God is making fun of us? He's satirizing all of our triumphal entries. He's paradying all of our parades. He's laughing at all of our strutting, preening, prideful pomp and circumstance. He's saying: "This is the kind of thing you enjoy, my children." And what does it all come to? Nothing! You have forgotten one important word in your ancient prophecy of Zechariah that you now see being fulfilled. You have forgotten the one important word, *"Behold, your King comes to you humble," – HUMBLE – "and sitting on an ass's colt."*

‡‡‡‡‡

New Testament Texts

MATTHEW 4:1-11

"And Jesus . . . tempted by the devil." Do you mean Jesus had trouble keeping his mind on God? *"He was tempted as we are,"* boasts Hebrews, *in every way."* It was no clinch for him to hold his temper, nor like falling off a log to hang on to his ideals. Are you saying, "He had to struggle to cling to the straight and narrow?" It was, according to the record, a struggle to the death.

Men have rebuilt Christ into an unhuman machine painlessly grinding out good deeds, so that we can't picture him standing in our shoes, sent into the ring himself with lust, or even wrestling with social approval, or floored by the blues. Today we go backstage to see that he went through hell. His test was not copies from divinity's paper — he dug out the answers himself.

His war against the Monster makes our moral scuffles seem child's play. God sent him to the front to lead the attack. We gripe about what we have to give up for "goodness sake." He paid capitol punishment and "like a lamb led before its shearers is dumb, so he opened not his mouth." We could not have lasted in the wilderness to which he was taken and would have been starved out before Beelsebub ever got there, long before the forty days were up. We have not carried our fight to the Mt. Everest he did. He faced gales at his altitude, as Dr. Fosdick said, that would have blown us off. The Devil had scouted this man as the one to nail or lose his Empire.

Christ knew more about temptation than any shady character ever did. As C.S. Lewis asks: "Who knows the Devil better? His victim or his conqueror?" We don't stuff our dirty linen down the drain, but send it to a laundry. So the church is not a Club for snow-white Angels but an ultraviolet school to decontaminate grimy miners and make them soldiers. It is not set up by the naive, but by the veteran Ace who has been through the mill and come back champion.

"And Jesus full of the Holy Spirit . . . tempted." Is it possible that evil could coax Christ as he was coming up out of the water of his baptism? Beelsebub hits hardest when the halo's brightest. Isn't Monday our low? His Infernal Majesty is waiting for us at the first break we take after communion. He times his visits to follow in the backwash of God's so he can have the last word while we have that letdown feeling.

Screwtape sat down before the dove's standing place was cold. He was in a better bargaining position, ready to bribe with a better offer — briefed, able to smear what was in the contract with the Almighty. "Are you sure it was God?" He rattles, "How do you know your ideal is not an 'Old Wives Tale?' " "You are not going to let your promising life be boxed in by that old black myth, are you?" "Come, come, straight lace will do for the old fashioned, or if you're frightened, but you are a very special case." "Don't you think a Cross is a little high, I can make you a little better price." Satan steps in hard on the heels of Angels.

Christ struggled so fiercely with himself he forgot his food for forty days. At last when he was starving the devil insinuated: *"If you are the son of God, command this stone to become bread."* Lucifer waited till Christ was tottering with exhaustion then smacked him hard in the pit of the stomach. But the Tempter stretched the offer to the man, not only tantalizing Christ with his next meal, but teasing him with the more inviting prospect of feeding the hungry masses everywhere.

But he was God's Son, not the Grocer's boy. It takes more than soup to satisfy men. Even porridge must be seasoned with something stronger before men will share their bowl. Christ must serve more than the head-waiter. Men must eat, but they are not here to eat. They can live without bread, but not without God's bread. Carlyle said:

"Not all the finance ministers, and the upholsterers and confectioners of modern Europe . . . in stock company, could make one shoe black happy above an hour or two." [*Interpreter's Bible, Vol. VII,* p. 271] "The famished Bedouin," George Buttrick of Harvard reports, "finding treasure in the desert, cried: 'Alas, it is only diamonds.' Men hunger and thirst for righteousness and cry at the dinner table: 'Alas, it is only bread.' "

No. Blaming economics for man's predicament was to be the Bolshevist blunder. Christ was not callous to the children's cries for milk, but that was a symptom of the heartbreaking sob in the spirit he must attend to first. He steadied himself and spoke through swollen lips: *"It is written man shall not live by bread alone but by every word that proceedeth from the mouth of God."*

Then the serpent placed his second bid. He showed Christ all the kingdoms of the world in a moment of time then announced: *"If you then will worship me, all this will be yours."*

This temptation is not wishful thinking. Christ actually faced this choice. Men clamored to crown him. Many another dictator has been swept into power with less ground swell. The time as ripe, for discontent was rife under Rome. The solid citizens were already looking around for their promised Military Messiah — his disciples rooting for him to take over. This hook was not baited by his imagination, the crowd was out there waiting for the word from him that would trigger the rebellion.

The temptation must have been terrific! What would be wrong with accepting the Presidency of such an ideal republic as he would establish? How that youth must have longed for such a tangible occupation — work he could get his hands on — see — show results. How irresistably this crown glowed out there in the desert, just out of reach. How exasperating was the drab alternative to this red blood. The job God had for him would start seed small and go snail slow — "If he was the son of God." Perhaps the baptism was a hoax, God's Voice faked by his overworked fancy. Who else would believe he was king without the robes? How could he do what he had to do without an army, the white horse? Was God going to make him the laughingstock of all times — or was God at all? What went on out there in the desert? Thirst nagged him — so did doubt.

Catlike, the tempter watched his trap. Now if Jesus could get down on his knees at Satan's feet. He couldn't stand. But he couldn't stand that. God's ways are not our ways. To use those methods would be to travel a polluted river to a lake of poison. He turned his back on the devil's expediency and came back with words that came from childhood. *"It is written, 'Thou shalt worship the Lord Thy God, and Him only shalt Thou serve.' "*

Failing to trip him on the first two tries, Satan finally threw in his feature attraction; *"And took Jesus to Jerusalem and set him on the pinnacle of the temple, telling him, 'If you are the Son of God, throw yourself down from here; for it is written he will give his angels charge over you.' "*

The Devil was acting now as if he were beaten. As if to say, "All right — you win. I believe you really are God's Son. Now let's let everybody in on it, too, by some dramatic exhibition." "Jump off a high place." God will let you down easily. That will capture everyone's attention and win their confidence with one stroke. Then, to cast his lure a little more lusciously, Satan got off a line or two of Scripture himself.

Men still can't find the holes in this one. What harm is there in proving Christianity by pointing to the spectacular? Something sensational is needed to get belief off the ground. The Devil, of course, was daring Christ to place himself in peril, so people could see God running to the rescue personally. Trick the Almighty into being seen.

How dazzling this idea must have been to an unknown, uneducated, stable born, countrybred carpenter. Mighty Moses had had his "staff into snake" trick, and a bulging pocketful of plagues to influence one Pharoah. But he knew better. It made him strong enough to say in that last crucial round: *"It is said, 'Thou shalt not tempt the Lord Thy God.' "*

Then the devil retreated — until the next opportunity. Christ had chased Satan from the field, but he would never be able to let down his guard. The Guerrilla would dog his trail to the end, retreat only to get him to turn his back. Satan even seduced Peter to try and rock Christ loose from his path. But he detected the fifth column and exorcized it: *"Get thee behind me Satan."* Then up ahead was Gethsemane. Would Satan never let him alone? Not til it was finished.

But rewarding recesses followed every campaign period. *"Then the devil leaveth him and behold Angels came and ministered unto him."* Temptation's no disgrace, if you win. God awards every loyal soldier after each battle. What is beseiging you now? An acid tongue, a promotion vs. integrity, the green eyed monster? Hold on tight — keep your mind on those things you've been taught held Christ unwavering — or learn them then. Temptation is bloody, but never hopeless — with his help — and a blessing worth the effort up ahead. The strains of victory will throb in the exultance of the heart and swell from a deep content. And you may feel, if not hear, wings.

"And Jesus returned in the power of the Spirit to Galilee." It was these early campaigns against hell that made a man of Christ — a God. You too. Every time you say "NO" makes it easier the next time. Every blow you make against evil strengthens your arm. Resisting the devil transfigures us "from strength to strength." Our trial is slow, at other times a storm of "touch and go." There is pain and the decisions always close. But if we stand fast now we shall be able to take the storm when it hits, and may, like Pilgrim, become "valiant," when our time comes, "gainst all disaster."

*****

Some have thought that since Jesus was the Son of God that his temptation must not have been very real. That he went through with it largely to set his followers an example. True, he did set us a great pattern; nevertheless his struggle was very, very real.

Jesus was baptized not only with water, but also with the Holy Spirit. Now he must soon begin his public ministry. Having now realized fully that he was to be the Messiah, he must take time to think it over and decide what kind of a Messiah he should be. At least 500 years the people of his day had been subject to foreign powers and this was considered to be not only a political but also a religious disgrace. So the people were looking for the Messiah to be, not a suffering Servant, but a materialistic conqueror of political and economic enemies!

No doubt Jesus had heard all through his life the longings and expectations of the people saying: "When the Messiah comes he will do marvelous things. He will feed us like Moses did in the wilderness. He will perform great miracles and above all he will raise a great army with supernatural power and he will break the power of Rome and set up the kingdom as it was in the days of David and Solomon." Thus Jesus was tempted to conform to the desires of the people. And he knew that if he didn't meet their expectations they would turn against him and crucify him. But Jesus met these temptations, "and what he determined in the mountain of temptations he went out to preach in the hills of Galilee." (Mary Austin)

‡‡‡‡‡

MATTHEW 15:21-28

"SEND HER AWAY FOR SHE IS CRYING AFTER US . . . O WOMAN, GREAT IS YOUR FAITH!"

Literally our Lord could have said to the Canaanitish

woman: "O woman, great is your persistence," because this was the quality of personality that she was displaying, the tenacity with which she presented her case before Christ. Nothing that he could say, even insulting her as a pagan, would drive her away from him. She was persistent, and she was successful. One is reminded of Paul when he writes: *"I have my own hardships to bear, even to being chained like a criminal, but they cannot chain up God's news."* [*2 Timothy 2:9*] This is the model of Christian persistence. Author Harry Golden once wrote: "If studies had been taken in the Roman Empire in 65 A.D. on religious preferences, they would have shown fifty-one percent for Jupiter, thirty percent for Zeus, about nine percent for Mithra and about one percent for Jesus." So St. Paul might just have gone home and said, "To hell with it," but Paul stayed, and that made the difference.

The persistence of the Canaanitish woman suggests the classic Greek comedy, *Lysistrata.* In the play the husbands of the woman of Athens persistently wage war against the Spartans. The women demand peace, but there is not peace. Then the heroine, Lysistrata, hits upon an ingenius plan. The woman will deny their husbands conjugal rights until they stop the killing. Says Lysistrata: "For if we women will but sit at home, powdered and trimmed, clad in our daintiest lawn, employing all our charms and all our arts to win men's love and when we've won it, then repel them firmly till they end the war, we'll soon get peace again. Be sure of that." As we all know, the plan worked, because of the persistence of the women.

*****

The following thank you letter appeared in the publication of a Roman Catholic religious order well known for conducting popular Novena Services. It is an example of misguided persistence. The letter read: "Dear Fathers: Please publish my thanks to the sacred heart, the infant Jesus of Prague and to the Blessed Mother for many favors received, among them the obtaining of an auto driver's license for my nephew who has very, very poor vision. His business was dependent on his ability to drive his car. Signed Mrs. L.S., North Carolina." In due course, another Roman Catholic publication carried this witty reply: "Residents of North Carolina are warned to watch out for a devout nephew with thick glasses. Residents of heaven are asked to stop kidding license inspectors."

‡‡‡‡‡

MATTHEW 17:1-9

Jesus was nearing the close of his earthly ministry. The ordeal of the cross was not far away. All along Jesus believed he was to die on the cross, but as the time drew near he seemed to want further assurance from God that he was doing his will. So he took Peter, James, and John and went up on the slope of Mount Hermon, and the transfiguration was God's answer of assurance. Luke (9:28-29) says that they went up into the mountain to pray and as he was praying his face did shine and his garments became white as the light.

Then Moses and Elijah appeared and talked of Jesus. A cloud overshadowed them and God's voice was heard from the cloud. "This is my beloved Son, in whom I am well pleased; hear him." All his life Jesus had lived in harmony with God's will; now at this very important time, God showed his approval again.

If Jesus needed to seek God's will, certainly we should do the same. How may we know God's will for our lives? A good answer has been given — do what is in harmony with the word of God, the Spirit of God, and the providence of God. The providence of God is revealed usually by closed and open doors. One of Paul's experiences illustrates this. When the door closed for any further preaching in Asia Minor, then the door opened in Macedonia, when he had the vision and the voice saying, "Come over into Macedonia and help us." He entered that door and later went on to Rome, but not until he had launched the Christian mission into a whole continent!

*****

The voice of God saying, "This is my beloved Son, hear him" must have been intended for Peter, James and John, and then later on they could convey this truth to the rest of the disciples. The Jewish people in Jesus' day including the disciples were looking for a warrior Messiah, not a suffering Servant. The voice of God must have been very convincing to them.

So we need the willingness to do God's will in our lives, and Jesus promised that the Holy Spirit would lead unto his truth. (John 16:13)

*****

In the last verse of the lesson, Jesus warns the disciples to tell the vision to no man until the Son of Man was risen from the dead. The reason for this request was that the people were so desirous of a warrior Messiah that they would misinterpret him and would begin to start revolutions against Rome, and Jesus' redemptive work as the Messiah would be thwarted.

So, as his disciples today, we need to know what and what not to say. We must not be contentious, argumentative, disputatious, but speak the truth with love and understanding of what is the truth of God.

‡‡‡‡‡

MATTHEW 20:17-28

1. We go up to Jerusalem [*Matthew 20:18*]

Here is a living example of fearlessness, of unwavering loyalty, and of determination to finish a task. At Jerusalem an ugly cross was waiting to inflict its cruel anguish upon Christ. Yet without flinching or hesitation he set his jaw and started for the city. Here was discipline of the first order, and an example to every follower of Christ.

Discipline is not popular today. The discipline of the armed forces is being eroded. Children are not to be warped by domination and so permissiveness runs full sway. "I want to be free." "I want to do my thing." These are the cries of many who are rebelling against the growth of character and talent that can come only when we bring ourselves under control. Ministering to this lack of discipline is the modern advertising that heralds "six easy lessons" to learn a foreign tongue or master a musical instrument. A book on camping was entitled "Roughing It Smoothly." That is the motto of modern life. But the worthwhile things come only at the cost of self-indulgence. The discipline of Christ calls on us to deny ourselves and take up our cross. And he made himself the great example. Only by a cross could God's plan of salvation be fulfilled. Other places beckoned; they offered him a crown, not a cross. But Christ went up to Jerusalem. Do we follow in his train?

2. What makes you angry? [*Matthew 20:24*]

The disciples were irritated by a mother whose love for her sons induced her to ask a favor of Christ on their behalf. The disciples were indignant when they heard of it. But these same men were soon thereafter to stand by, or flee, without venting their indignation while Christ was maligned, beaten and put to death. One of the tests of a man or woman is what stirs him to anger. The self-centered individual is stirred to ire when anything disturbs his comfort, but the suffering of his fellow man, or great social injusties do not even jar him. Our irritability is not necessarily bad. It is the level at which it appears that is important. Even Christ became irritable at times and vented his indignation against those who perverted the temple or were hypocritical. Use this as a measurement of yourself: What is it that stirs you to anger?

3. Service is the way to honor [*Matthew 20:27*]

Once a clergyman wrote an article for a magazine that attracted considerable attention. It was entitled "Why I Do Not Want My Son to Become a Minister." In the article he stressed how many are the demands made upon a minister and stated that he wanted his son spared these irritating requests for help. Another minister commended that the title of the article should have been "Why I Want My Son to be Ministered Unto, Not to Minister." In the Scriptures Christ himself is pictured as a servant. He stated, furthermore, that the degree to which his followers would be honored by the heavenly Father depended on how much they, too, were committed to being servants of the Lord. In John Wolman's Diary we read how that great man was severely disturbed on a visit to the various societies of Friends in North Carolina. The cause of his distress was the constant entry in the minutes of their meetings of the phrase: "No business that required entry." This moved him to comment, "In God's name, why was there not some business that required entry and strong action? With the sin of slavery and its cruelties all around them, and the sin of war impending, how could they say, 'No business that required entry'?" For the Christian, the business of service in Christ's name is always at hand.

‡‡‡‡‡

MATTHEW 21:1-11

1. The Master needs them [*Matthew 21:2*]

There is much talk of priorities today, the placing of things in their proper order of importance, with first things coming first. When Christ needed the donkey to ride into Jerusalem, it was enough to say to the owner that the Master needed the beast. Christ was to have first call on its use, as a matter of course. This should be the case in Christ's requests of us. The proper priority in life is Christ first, others second, selves third. Unfortunately, most people reverse the order. They are like the curious animal called a sloth which lives in trees and spends most of its time living upside down. They hang from their tails with their head nearest the ground, whether sleeping, eating or even at times when moving about. Do we have, at the top of our priority list, those things which deserve to enjoy first place, or are they on the bottom? It was said of the early disciples that they turned the world upside down. They were simply restoring spiritual and moral values to their rightful priority. On the basis of this judgment, are we, too, disciples of Christ?

2. The triumphant Christ [*Matthew 21:9*]

Roman generals, returning from highly successful campaigns of military conquest, were given enthusiastic welcome by the large crowds who turned out to celebrate their victor. In every nation, after each successful military holocaust, the return of the conquerors is hearlded with much pomp and the enthusiasm of large crowds. At the close of the War between the States, the Army of the Potomac and the Army of Sherman marched down Pennsylvania Avenue. They passed the reviewing stand where General Grant, President of the United States, was standing. Similar parades have followed World War I and II with such crowds present that it took days for workmen to clear the streets of debris in New York and Washington. But while the Palm Sunday procession was equally impressive, it was entirely different. It celebrated a greater and grander triumph. It did not mark the conquest of other nations but of human hearts. It celebrated the Lord of Life, not the slaughter of war. This was the Prince of Peace. Now they publicly recognized him as the Son of God. He is the conqueror of our greatest enemies: sin and death. He must ride in triumph in our hearts and be forever hailed as King of kings and Lord of lords.

3. Some threw down their coats along the way [*Matthew 21:8*]

Although not done today, it was long the custom of people to greet a hero by throwing a piece of one's clothing in his path to walk upon. In ancient times this was done for Jehu when he was made leader of the army of Israel. It was done for Christ by people who were acquainted with the practice. The gallant act of Sir Walter Raleigh, in spreading his beautiful cape on the muddy ground for Queen Victoria to walk upon, is well known.

We do not have the opportunity to stand in a great throng and greet Christ by throwing a garment in the road. But we are to carry out a quite similar gesture. We are to give up our treasures, our time and talents and money, and lay them at his feet. By acts of love we are to prepare a way for him to win human hearts. In this way we will appreciate in his grand, triumphal march through the ages.

*****

"AND THE CROWDS THAT WENT BEFORE HIM AND THAT FOLLOWED HIM SHOUTED: 'HOSANNA TO THE SON OF DAVID. BLESSED IS HE WHO COMES IN THE NAME OF THE LORD.' "

It was a queer day in that far-off, long distant day in Judea. It was a day of contrasts of light and shadow, of climax and anticlimax, of frustration and fulfillment, of tears and hosannas. Yes, it was a queer kind of day, just as queer as life. The key to it, I think, occurred back in the brief moment when Jesus, rounding a bend in the road, saw the city nestled in its hills like a jewel in a setting, and looking down over that city, he broke down and wept: *"Oh, Jerusalem, Jerusalem, if thou hadst only known, at least in this thy day, the things that belong unto thy peace, but now they are hid from thine eyes."*

From that moment on, from the moment that Jesus arrived triumphantly in the city and DID NOTHING, his fate was sealed. Just five days later, the palms of trees had turned into the palms of hands. No hosannas now, just the snarling taunts: "All right, you're the Messiah. You're the King of the Jews. Then prophesy! Who struck you? Who struck you? Oh, I know there is blood in your eyes from that stupid crown on your head, so you can't see, but you shouldn't have to see. Remember, you're the Son of God. Who struck you?"

Who hit him, friends? Oh, don't turn away. I'm talking to you. Who hit him? We were in that crowd, too, you know. We still are. We've come to wave our palms and shout our hosannas. Why? Come on, let's dig down deep where we really live inside here. Who's getting himself worshipped here? Who's supposed to be the recipient of all of this glory? Who's supposed to be getting the most out of this show? Why did the singing worshippers become a bloodthirsty lynching mob? You say they were fickle? No, that's the hell of it. They weren't fickle at all. They were frighteningly, devilishly, horribly consistent. They hadn't changed one iota in five days. They were still there for the same purpose, for what THEY could get out of it. They were still there worshipping the same god — themselves. They were still putting first things first — yours truly.

*****

Well, fellow palm wavers, what about us? Are we any different? There will be big crowds in church this morning, and many hosannas will be sung. So you say: "O.K., preacher, don't kick it. This is what you want, isn't it? We're here. We're singing. We're worshipping. What else do you want?" Well, it's like the teacher who sent the little boy home with a note to his mother. "Johnny is very dirty. He smells. Please give him a bath." The mother wrote back: "Johnny ain't no rose. Don't smell him. Learn him something." But, unfortunately, I have to stand here in the place of the prophet Isaiah. I have to give you the Word of God as Isaiah quoted it: *"I hate your feasts and your worship. The smoke of your sacrifices and the smell of your incense stinks up the heavens."* Why? *"Because it is not I," saith the Lord, "who is being worshipped."*

*****

A lady in the congregation complains to me: "I couldn't understand the words of the anthem." And I have to bite my tongue so that I don't remind her that the anthem wasn't being sung to her, and I suspect that Almighty God understood the words. How often I hear the old excuse: "I don't come to church because I don't get anything out of it." That's putting it pretty bluntly, isn't it? That's telling the whole story in one sentence. Who said we were SUPPOSED to be getting anything out of it? Pray, who is being worshipped here? Or the question is: "Can't we sing some hymns I enjoy?" Well, it all depends upon whom the hymns are being sung to. "With all the money we spend on air conditioning, can't we keep this building comfortable?" Well, we can try, if being comfortable is what you come here for. "Don't expect me to sing. You wouldn't want to hear my voice." I probably wouldn't, but maybe Almighty God would. He gave you the voice. And so, Kierkegaard says: "We gather together for worship and pray together 'Thy will be done on earth as it is in heaven.' without the slightest concern for God's will except as it happens to coincide with our will."

Why are we here fellow palm wavers? We are like the elderly black gentleman who appeared at the gate of the White House shortly after the Civil War. He was carrying an empty basket. He told the guard: "I've been told that the Constitution has provisions for me, and I'm here to get mine." We've been told that the Christian faith has provisions for us, and we are here to get ours. And so we end up with a silent, do-nothing Christ.

*****

So we take over. If he isn't going to get us what we want in life, then we'll do it ourselves. If he isn't going to lead us into peace, power, poise, and prosperity, then we'll get it for ourselves. If he isn't going to be our leader, our King, our Messiah, then we'll have our own. Henry van Dyke has some lines about our attempt to do this:

"One day God said, 'I'm tired of kings,'
But that was long ago,
And man kept saying, No.
I like their looks in robes and rings,
So He crowned a few more.
And the kings as before
Kept fighting and spoiling things.
But at last man said, 'I'm tired of kings,
Sons of the robber, chiefs of yore,
They make me pay for their lust and their war.
I am the puppet, they pull the strings,
The blood of my heart is the wine they drink.
I shall govern myself for a while, I think,
And see what that brings.
Then God [who had made the first remark]
Smiled in the dark."

‡‡‡‡‡

MARK 16:1-7

"HE HAS RISEN"

It was a solid, staid, old parish to which I was called just after the war, one that needed a bit of waking up here and there, and on our first Easter, we arranged to have the Sunrise Service begin with a fanfare by a quartet of trumpets sounding forth from the balcony. Well, the trumpeters were quite enthusiastic, and I must admit, quite loud; and, quite frankly, the innovation was not received with unanimous approval. In fact, one elderly lady in the congregation was quite vocal about it. She said: "I don't mind some changes. After all, you have to expect that with a young, new pastor, but trumpets in the church on Easter, the very idea! That's carrying things a bit too far." Well, bless her soul, like a lot of other pinch-mouthed Christians, she hadn't read her Bible carefully enough to discover that the new pastor wasn't being particularly original with the trumpet bit. A preacher by the name of Paul, you see, beat me to it by quite a few centuries. He put it this way: "For the trumpet shall sound and the dead shall be raised; then shall be brought to pass the saying that is written, 'Death is swallowed up in victory.' " Trumpets — the sound of victory! And Paul concludes that glorious chapter, the 15th of his First Letter to the Corinthians, with these words: "Thanks be to God who giveth us the victory through our Lord Jesus Christ."

*****

Quite a crowd that has gathered here this morning, isn't it? Tell me, why did you all come? Why have we crowded, not only this, but every Christian church throughout the world? Why the throngs on Easter morning? No, don't say it. I know what you're going to say, and I don't believe it. I've heard all of the cynical answers. I've heard all of the reasons that the skeptics and the critics of the church have given, and I don't believe them. I've read all the cracks by the bright boys with the fast quip, and I'm not buying it for a minute. Do you want a revue? All right. You come out of social conformity. Coming to church on Easter is just like getting bagged on New Year's Eve. It's the thing to do. Everybody does it, and so you do it. Or perhaps you have come to see and be seen. Where else would you have such a wide audience for your new spring wardrobe? Or perhaps because it is spring. The weather isn't good enough to play golf or have a picnic, and there doesn't seem much else to do on a morning like this, and so you came to church. Or maybe you can't really call yourself religious or a good member of the church, but you like to keep some connection, and a once a year visit to the church seems to sort of fill the bill in that regard. And to all of this I say: "Bunk! Rubbish! Unmitigated balderdash! I don't believe it for a moment." Just twenty-six years ago this Easter, I had all of this nonsense debunked for me. It was Easter Sunday. Two days before, we had left the island of Iwo Jima. For thirty days, since we had landed on the beach of that island, we had lived with death — the sight of it, the sound of it, the scream of it, the stench of it. Death! For nearly a month, we had witnessed death in its most violent, its most sudden, its most futile, its most bloody, its most debasing ways. For days, we had collected bodies, we had burned bodies, we had carried bodies, we had buried bodies. And so we gathered for our Easter Service. It wasn't in any lovely lily-bedecked sanctuary such as this. It was a smelly mess hall below decks aboard a transport ship. There were no lovely ladies in bright millinery. The dress was dirty dungarees. There was not fine choir with inspiring music. We sang the Easter hymns to the accompaniment of a squeaky, little, portable, reed organ. No one told anyone he had to come. There was no social custom or conformity about it. And yet, that mess hall was jam-packed with men. There wasn't a square inch of space that wasn't taken. There were many who didn't get in, and we couldn't go topside on deck, because we were riding out a typhoon, which made it even a little less like an Easter. I looked out on men with red-rimmed eyes, with beards, with bandages. Al right, my wise skeptic. Why did they come? It was best put by a Marine after the Service, when he said: "Well, Padre, I guess after all that back there, we just had to come this morning, didn't we?" And I'll say that for all of us today: after all of that back there, we just had to come this morning. After another year on this bloody earth, we had to come. There was no alternative. We needed this desperately, this Easter celebration. Every day of this past year has been covered by a pall of death that has hung over it like a dark cloud. It seemed we could never escape. It was in the weekly box score of casualties from Viet Nam, and even if we came out ahead in the totals for the week, we still couldn't muster up much joy about it, because some wife, or some mother, or some son had lost a man whom they loved. Friend or enemy, which did it matter? It was death.

With every breath we take, someone is dying somewhere in the world. Why don't we get used to it? Psychologists tell us that a child at the age of six becomes aware of death. The naturalist tells us that it's just a normal part of life. He says it, but he doesn't believe it, and neither do we. To coin the terrible contradiction — we live with death. And so we have come to celebrate the resurrection. This is the normal thing to do! We need to see the Risen Christ standing before us. What would you have me do this morning? Build some kind of a solid, skilled, scholarly statement and documentation for the resurrection of Jesus Christ? You wouldn't want that, even if I could. Your presence here is proof enough of that resurrection. I remember asking a young widow if there was anything in particular that she wanted me to include in the Service for her husband. She said: "No, just go out there and tell me again that this isn't the end of everything." That's what we all want to know this morning. There's something else we need to know. Paul says it: "We are risen with Christ now. We have eternal life now." Today, that's what we want verified. A layman friend of mine was describing the dullness of his own pastor's sermons. He said: "He has the unique ability to make twenty minutes seem like an eternity." Well, in a sense, that is what I'm supposed to do this morning. In a few, brief minutes, I'm supposed to make you feel like you are living eternal life. That's that you want, but life as we live it is so small, so futile, so restricted, so provincial, it seems we're forever beating our heads against the walls that surround us. We know so much, and yet, we know so little about the world because we're confined to such a small place. We're like the woman whose brother during World War II was sent to the continent down under. He decided to stay there and live. One day she was going to the zoo, and she was standing in front of the kangaroo cage. She read the sign: "Native of Australia." "Good heavens!" she gasped, "my brother married one of them." Little lives that never get beyond little surroundings in a little place. They don't seem very eternal, do they?

*****

"Who will roll away the stone for us from the door of the tomb?" [*Mark 16:3*]

This is a wonderful life except for the stone of death staring us in the face. There are other stones. Each man seems to have his own stone weighing on his chest, or around his neck. It is always too heavy for us to handle alone. We are entombed except for outside help. We are already in our graves unless God brings us back to life better than ever.

Guideposts for February, 1964, tells the story of miners trapped by an underwater lake draining into their pit.

I had just gone back into No. 1 room when it happened. Over the rattle of machinery I heard Frank Scarbro's yell. "Larry! Boys! Come on! There's water in here!"

It roared out of No. 3 room in what seemed like a solid wall, knocking down support timbers, tearing up huge slabs of slate.

"Up here," Frank's voice called again. "There's a high ground here." I crawled toward him. Six of us gathered there. That meant that four men were missing. We waded out to the edge of the tunnel, shouting to the missing men above the roar, shining our lamps in every direction. Nothing. We struggled back to the higher ground and sat there close to one another, wet, scared, cold to the bone, listening to the torrent pound past. For two hours it rushed by, never slacking, never falling, filling up the worked-out areas below us, then rising to seal off the mouth of the room where we sat.

"Looks like we're going to be here for a while, men," John Moore said, and I'm sure that more than one of us had the temptation to say, "Maybe forever." But we didn't say it — not aloud anyway. We set about instead to make as safe a place for ourselves as we could.

Blackdamp was one of the main dangers we faced. Blackdamp is the deadly odorless gas of the mines, and it can get you down before you know it's there. In a corner we found a roll of brattice cloth — treated burlap — and used it to barricade ourselves against possible blackdamp. With the water still roaring past in the tunnel, we made a tent of the brattice cloth and crawled inside.

Now we took stock of our food supply. Two lunch pails had been saved. There were a few sandwiches, four or five candy bars and some cake. That wouldn't last long among six men. But the chances were the water would get us before we got very hungry.

And then I remembered the story of Daniel. The day before, Sunday, after church, I'd had the strongest feeling that God was telling me to read the Bible, just to let it fall open at random. So I'd done it, and where should it open but to the story of how God brought Daniel out of the lion's den.

"Listen, fellows," I said. "Listen to what God told me just yesterday." I couldn't remember the exact words, I said, but they had to do with the way God 'delivereth and rescueth and worketh . . . wonders in heaven and in earth.' [Dan. 6:27] "I think we ought to ask for a wonder in the earth," I said. And in that dark hole, we asked that the water stop rising.

But it didn't stop. Every hour or so someone would crawl out of the tent and go down to the water line. But the message was always the same. "It's over the last mark on the timber."

At the end of about 13 hours the water stopped its furious charge. We figured that the underground lake or whatever it was that we had tapped into, was finally drained. But still the water rose. Everyone was praying now — even men who'd never prayed before — but it seemed that the harder we prayed the faster that water crept up on us.

And then someone said suddenly, "They think we're drowned."

Now it was in words, the thought we'd all been dodging. "They're not hurrying, because there's no way anyone could be alive down here."

Nobody answered. All of us were thinking of the miner's tradition that now alone stood between us and death: the tradition that says rescue operations continue until not only the living but the dead are recovered.

And all the while the water rose.

Three days passed. Four. The water was almost halfway up the room. What was keeping it from the pocket where we were?

At the end of the fourth day our food ran out. Some of the men found crusts tossed aside by miners days before and wolfed down those scraps.

We hunched closer to each other to keep out the cold, not moving much, to conserve energy. And the water rose.

It was on the seventh day that I suddenly wondered if word prayers were enough. In the Bible, men didn't only say they believed, they acted like it. They went out and made bold, foolish, extravagant gestures to prove it.

I switched on my head lamp. "Boys," I said, "I'm going down to the water. Don't worry about me."

I crawled out of the tent. The water was at the highest point yet, still and black in the yellow light of my lamp. Little specks of coal dust swam lazily on the surface, going nowhere.

"Lord," I said, "You've given us the Bible not as ancient history but as a pattern for now. Give me the faith, Jesus, to receive a real Bible miracle."

I ran over in my mind everything I remembered about how Elijah and Moses divided the waters. What would happen if I commanded the waters to recede? There in the darkness of that flooded mine, God gave me the faith to ask for a miracle. I hit the water. I smote it five times with a piece of old conveyer chain, spelling out the name "Jesus" and I ordered the floods to draw back.

Then I knelt down at the water's edge. I waited for the waves I had created to die down, for the specks of coal dust to stop moving about.

It seemed to be taking too long. Why was it that the coal dust, instead of settling down, was now running together as it pulled by a little current? I picked out one speck and followed it. Could it be my imagination? No, that speck of dust was moving away from the water's edge. I watched for a while, almost unbelieving. For that water — that water was drawing back.

When it had dropped far enough to remove all doubt, I went back and told the others. Then I promised God that when we were rescued I'd not do one thing before I stood up in His great Openness and gave thanks.

On the eighth day we heard drilling. The bit broke

through the ceiling. But it was some hundred yards away from us, in the totally flooded tunnel. They'd take that as proof that no one in this section was alive.

The ninth day came and went. But we heard the sounds of pumping through the hold in the tunnel ceiling. By the tenth day we were too weak to do much but lie in the tent and rest.

And then, as it it were in a dream, suddenly there was a head lamp shining in through the bratice cloth, and a voice shouted, "Boys, you sure look good!"

It was night when they got us to the tunnel mouth. Even before we reached it, we smelled God's good sweet air. They wanted us to stay on the stretchers, but we'd been waiting ten days to stand up straight. In the glare of floodlights I saw my father and brother standing among others. Before we let them put us in the ambulance, four of us joined hands and lifted our arms, and there in the floodlights we gave thanks unto the Lord, our Deliverer.

Of course, eventually we all must die. Had the miners drowned, they would have still been eligible to have their tombs emptied. Jesus would have been waiting for them as for our fathers. This is the big news. The story of the mine gives us a glimpse of large miracle waiting for us all at death.

Think of the stone of gravity pressing down upon earth's chest. That stone has been rolled away and sent us flying into space. In a recent issue of *Time*, it was noted that the Apollo astronaut veterans have become changed men as a result of their "instant global consciousness."

Philosopher William Irwin Thompson, who perceives a growing sense of myth and mysticism in today's technological society, mused over the astronauts' "conversions" as he watched the ascent of Apollo 17. In space, Thompson says, the astronauts felt "their consciousness being transformed to behold God making all things new."

In a sense, argues Thompson, the astronauts underwent a kind of "temporal redemption, much like the one envisioned 34 years ago in C.S. Lewis' theological space fantasy OUT OF THE SILENT PLANET. In Lewis' novel, the earth is the devil's territory and the prison of fallen man, quarantined by the powers and dominations of the divine milieu around it. But those who escape the silent planet can recover their cosmic orientation. [*Time, August 21, 1972*]

Earth is not entombed in a stone of space. We are not limited to this atmosphere. This is a parable about death. The huge stone which so worried the women on their way to the tomb had already been rolled away. God does not weigh us down. He is the weight lifter.

‡‡‡‡‡

LUKE 4:1-13

No matter how many times I look at this text, I come back to my first inclination: "Temptations of Ministry." Each of the temptations can be related to temptations of the individual Christian or the corporate Christian body today. In a sermon based on that theme, you might make several points which may not be obvious to the worshiper who has just heard the Gospel read orally:

1. Jesus' temptation followed the "big" day of his Baptism when he learned his vocation. (You might even want to refer to the First Sunday after the Epiphany and the Luke 3 text.)

2. Each temptation involves that tricky little word "if" — hence, doubt as to his vocation is suggested to Jesus by the devil.

3. The devil himself presents a problem to many modern minds. That might be pause for serious consideration in the sermon. The Scriptures testify that the devil does exist. As you seek to portray the workings of the devil to contemporary Christians, recall

Shakespeare's familiar quote, "The prince of darkness is a gentleman."

C. S. Lewis, in *The Screwtape Letters,* has Screwtape, the senior devil in hell, tutoring his nephew on earth who is working on a human victim, write, "I wonder you should ask me whether it is essential to keep the patient in ignorance of your own existence . . . Our policy . . . is to conceal ourselves . . . I do not think you will have much difficulty in keeping the patient in the dark. The fact that 'devils' are predominantly *comic* figures in the modern imagination will help you. If any faint suspicion of your existence begins to arise in his mind, suggest to him a picture of something in red tights, and persuade him that since he cannot believe in that . . . he therefore cannot believe in you." (NY: Macmillan, 1961) There is merit in the suggestion that the 1977 concept of the devil is hardly different from the one for which Lewis wrote several decades ago.

Now to the temptations themselves. The first was a temptation to cheap substitutions. Jesus' answer, "Man does not live by bread alone," clearly indicates that more is needed in ministry than food for our stomachs. If the Church in our day feeds the hungry or tends to the physical needs of the poor and oppressed, simply to get them off our middleclass, gleaming hands, we are substituting for the real thing — proclamation of a relationship with Christ (Vertical) and with ourselves (Horizontal).

Further illustrations of succumbing to cheap substitutions in ministry abound in every parish: sending the church flowers, every once in a while, to the parish's elderly shut-ins, but not visiting them and developing relationship with them; insisting that there be a "strong youth program" but never involving ourselves in relationship with those youth, always letting "George" or a hired professional do it; treatment of the poor and oppressed as suggested above, particularly in urban settings; sending a proper card to a sick or bereaved fellow parishioner, but never involving ourselves in a relationship to the person to minister personally to him.

Second, Jesus was tempted to exercise political power to take the easy, seemingly most practical way, the way of expediency (which was precisely the way he was later dealt with by Caiaphas and company). In different words, Jesus was tempted to compromise, to let the end justify the means.

In contemporary life, the Christian individual and the Church are decidedly called upon to exercise political power — but under the love and justice of God. Individually the exercise of the ballot comes to mind, and we are called to scrutinize our reasons for voting yes or no for urban renewal, school bond issues, state lotteries, and the whole host of issues that come to us for decision. Our individual answers should be given based upon our sense of responsibility for the world God gave us to minister to.

Corporately, we need to address and act upon issues and persons around us with that same responsibility, so that we minister to the world, whether the issue is abortion or drug laws or political campaigns or what have you, without compromising. It would be well to keep in mind something which U.S. Senator Edward Long of Missouri said several years ago as we consider whether we are ministering or simply trying to force our own individual (and corporate) viewpoints on society: "Society is continually pushing in on the individual. He has only a few areas in which he can be himself, free from external restraint or observation."

Third, Jesus was tempted to be a showoff. "Convince me, by something spectacular, that you really are God's Son!" Many contemporary Christians continue to demand miracles when they want miracles — healing for example. Many, both within and outside the church, continue to demand this or that from the church as a contingency upon their membership and participation.

This temptation may also be seen as a strong drive for results — the American result-itis and seemingly insatiable hunger for bigger and better, where numbers and dollars rather than personal ministry and relationship count. No matter who says, "Show me by doing such and such," the contemporary church must be faithful to the ministry to which she is called and to the message she proclaims.

‡‡‡‡‡

LUKE 11:14-28

"BY MEANS OF GOD'S POWER, I DROVE OUT DEMONS."

One cannot go off drugs without going on something else. As penal officers know, getting a drunk off drink or an addict off drugs leaves the house empty and prey for a swarm of other demons. Sweeping out the Kaiser only made room for Hitler.

As Jesus explained in this Scripture: the only way to be rid of a demon for good is to crowd him out with the best. Don't leave any room for his return. The room will be filled. If you don't fill it with Windy Gap and good friends, it will attract vandals. Staying off drugs is not accomplished negatively. Get on Christ.

Our lives are like unruly frontiers. Lawbreakers bully the western town that has no competent marshall. And even if there is a posse and a successful shoot-out, more bad guys pour in.

Manitoba, Canada used to be a free-for-all territory. Nobody was tough enough to put it in order. Lawbreakers and six guns poured in. Every time it was swept out made more room for more. Finally Samuel Benfield Steele came. He was 22, so tall and thin he had to wear a sash under his tunic. He was promoted to inspector of the Northwest Mounted Police, and made them mounties. He trained them in 36 degrees below zero weather. He was ordered with a party of 25 horsemen to Calgary, Alberta to police the construction of the Canadian Pacific Railway. The riot came when he was sick in bed, but he got up and coldly faced a mob of flashing knives with a drawn pistol and singlehandedly faced down the mob at a narrow bridge. In the Canadian WHO WAS WHO there is this sentence about Samuel Steele. "His coming meant order. His presence meant justice. His name was worth a regiment." Doesn't that remind you of the name that is above every other name before whom every knee shall bow and every tongue confess?" Send for him for he is not far from any one of us. *"For the love of Christ controls us."*

‡‡‡‡‡

LUKE 15:1-3, 11-32

"At last he came to his senses," Luke writes in describing the dramatic turning point in the life of the young man whom we've come to call "the prodigal son." That, in *Today's English Version,* corresponds to RSV's "But when he came to himself." Whatever else, this one thing is clear: the young man was obviously not himself before. His friends would have said of him, "He's not himself these days." His grieving family would have claimed that he had flipped in an astonishing personality change. His acquaintances, a little more objective than others, would have cried, "What a fool he is!" But, then, when he came to his senses, he himself was saying, "What a fool I've been!"

When he came to his senses, this young man, who might have been a first century Palestinian playboy, suddenly realized and said aloud to himself — a point to remember — that he had been living in an unreal world; that, in his total self-concern, he was not really himself; that, isolated, he was simply non-human, incomplete, and alienated from that which gave his life meaning: his father's household.

No wonder, then, that his first thought when he came to his senses, was the thought to return home, to plead with his father for acceptance, not as a son, but as a hired servant. The independent, arrogant son, who thought he could go it alone, was brought so low that he was willing to crawl home . . . bent, drawn, scraggly . . . where once he had walked proudly, head high, in full command as the son of the master.

*****

The foregoing is suggested as a kind of "starter" for a sermon dealing with this text. Although the possibilities for preaching on this Lukan passage are many, an approach that appeals to me at this junction in our history is to speak God's Word on our own self-recognition. The younger son recognized who he was only when he realized that his identity was dependent upon his relationship to his father's household. He tried to escape that, but found his life ending up in a pig pen (imagine the horror of that to a first century Jew) when the *relationship* was broken.

The son came home to his father's household claiming to be only what he is — a lonely, meaningless man outside of that relationship. Such a sermon could include discussion of one's self-image as well. Surely, it would include reflection upon the father's *household*, as well as the Father, which permits a discussion of our relationship to the Father's other children. In the discussion, we should not be timid in pointing out that coming to the recognition of our identity is sometimes painful.

The good news in this text, of course, is that the father is waiting to bestow our identity upon us again — at least from our point of view, for, from his he's not removed it — when we come to our senses and recognize that we are what we are because we belong to the family of God and to the family of man (the father's household).

The good news is hilarious! The father received his wandering son in an hilarious way, when you think about it. The son received back all that he thought he had forsaken when he wandered into a far country. Henry Wheeler Shaw wrote, "Love looks through a telescope; envy through a microscope." The father's telescopic vision gave him a perspective of love on the son. The elder brother's envy was microscopic vision — scrutinizing, self-righteously, for flaws in both his younger brother and in his father's treatment of that brother.

*****

An alternate suggestion: If you want to do something dramatically different with this text, get two others to join you in a trialogue in which, after careful discussion of the text and careful planning, you stage a scene (in the modern vein) on the porch of the father's house during the party he gives for the returning son. The two brothers are in a discussion of what has taken place — and the elder is self-righteous, even vindictive. The younger is bewildered and overwhelmed by the reception. The father comes out and, upon verbal attack by the older brother, talks about his love for both. I did this once, quite successfully; but a warning: it does take careful preparation.

‡‡‡‡‡

LUKE 20:9-19

Judgment! It's here, straight-out, not couched, not hesitant. In its contemporary application, this parable speaks a word of judgment to Christian congregations/individuals today, with the same message: our discipleship and stewardship in the Lord's world (vineyard) is sadly lacking!

The best illustrations for a sermon on this text which would seek to pronounce prophetic judgment *and* point the way to a more responsible congregational ministry will come from each individual's own unique circumstances. What I'd like to offer here are some quotations which, even if not used in a sermon, could help spark sermon points for at-home examples of our rejection of the Christ when we thwart renewal or hamper genuine mission; when we seek success, prestige, respectability, and bigger budgets and buildings to impress; when we snub those who are different in our society; when we resist change just because we like it the way it's "always been."

*****

"Each parish, if it is to have a legitimate existence, will work to minister to the center of people's lives instead of the tangents. If it works only with their private and family lives, it must reach to the central human needs . . . The typical overly busy parish contents itself with touching the many edges of people's lives, entertaining them or occupying them in trivial tasks. What they need and deserve from a Christian ministry is a basic way of looking at what life and eternity demand and offer them."

Martin Marty

*****

Dr. Harold Williams, Provost, Coventry Cathedral, England: *The church must help find common factors between the young and the old, the black and the white, etc. It must help members of these different groups see each other as MEN, to get them off their collision courses. People are on collision courses all the time. The church must get them to talk about it.*

*****

One of the most beautiful sights you can see at night, from the great heights that a jet plane can reach, is the many-splendored brightness, the rainbow-hued glow of a great city. And it comes as an awful letdown, when you land in that city, to realize that the beautiful glow in the night sky came from the garish and gaudy neon signs, shrieking out their cacophony of "Blatz Beer" and "Harry's Tavern," and "Eat, Drink, Dance."

That experience, which many have had, seems to suggest to me the experience that many have of the Church. We proclaim a glowing message, yet when people come to us to see what it's all about they are keenly disappointed in the reality of a church life that does not live what it professes or minister as it is called to do.

*****

In *The Comfortable Pew*, Pierre Berton wrote, "The church, to its opponents, has become a straw man scarcely worth a bullet." It's "a pasttime for people who like that sort of thing."

‡‡‡‡‡

JOHN 6:1-15

"AND SO THEY GATHERED THEM UP AND FILLED TWELVE BASKETS WITH FRAGMENTS FROM THE FIVE BARLEY LOAVES LEFT BY THOSE WHO HAD EATEN"

One pastor writes: "During World War II, I served as a Chaplain in the Armed Services. I well recall an incident that happened as I traveled by train from Gloucester, England to London. The English trains have compartments, like American railroad cars, and each compartment holds six to eight persons. Before leaving Gloucester, I was given a C-Ration by our Mess

Sergeant. We had boarded the train about 9:00 a.m. Noontime, lunch time came and went, and by 1:30 P.M., I was quite hungry and wished that I dared eat my lunch. No one else had eaten, and so I had not. I decided that I would solve the problem by sharing my C-Ration with the five other persons in that compartment. I took out the small can of cheese, cut it into six sections. The pack also included six 'dog biscuits' and a small candy bar. (No one had talked all morning, but all were watching my preparations for eating.) I turned to a well-dressed matron on my right and offered her a piece of cheese and candy. She became talkative immediately, thanked me, but she had lunch, too. She proceeded to get it out of a basket. Likewise with the four other persons. We all had lunches, and, quite obviously, all were hungry, but none had had the gall to eat in the presence of others who might not have lunches. What a good time we all had from that time on. When I stepped off the train in London, I had two beef sandwiches, several pieces of homemade candy, an orange, and a piece of cake. My supper was ready. My thoughts raced excitedly. I thought of the feeding of the five thousand, and I had a hint as to what might have happened. The selfish had become unselfish. The hesitant to share had opened their meager supplies and shared with those around them. Concern and love had opened resources unthought of." There is an old saying, "There is not enough for everybody's greed. There is enough for everybody's need."

Why the twelve baskets full of leftovers? Why all the garbage? Was out Lord just pulling a kind of grandstand trick to titillate the crowd? Was he just engaging in poor management, as far as food efficiency was concerned? Not so! He was doing the customary — the abundance of God, his extravagance. As the poet Allen Watts has put it:

Oh, the tremendous quantities —
God's extravagance, to be found
In the unnecessary vastness of nature."

Yes, we know that other nations have had to stand the test of privation, want, pain, fear, bloodshed, warfare, disruption, slavery. But we face another kind of test and a much more terrible temptation. God's extravagant kindness to us may be his most demanding test of our love and loyalty. In the *Saturday Review* almost an entire issue was spent on the American economy. There were two lead articles, one by Leo Cherne, the Executive Director of the Research Institute of America; and the other by Kenneth Boulding, Professor of Economics at Colorado University. The titles of the articles were revealing. Mr. Cherne calls his "The Trillion Dollar Frustration," and he states that President-Elect Nixon will be able to announce to the people of the United States that we have reached a trillion dollars (that is a staggering figure. I don't even know what it means) — "a trillion dollars Gross National Products." But then he states the frustration. He lists the economic problems that will face the President — balance of international payments, budget deficits, costs of armament, foreign aid, the stagnant alliance for progress, the United States and the Common Market, the inadequate base of international exchange, massive Federal debts and carrying charges, price stability, reconstruction in Vietnam, tariff policy and foreign competition, and the Asian famine that is due some time in the 70's, the shrinking U.S. gold reserves, the aged, the chronic poor, education, medical care, population growth, unemployment, agricultural subsidies, decaying ghettos, pollution, inflation. Then he asks: "Can a nation with a trillion dollar Gross National Product plead poverty when it comes to meeting our social needs?"

*****

Mr. Boulding calls his article "The Many Failures of Success." He said: "Our overall success in our economy is nothing less than uproarious. We have not had a serious depression in twenty years. We have had the longest continuous upsurge in our economy in history. Looking at the figures, we can hardly say anything except 'Hallelujah.' We are the world's richest nation, and we are going to be that for some time to come, but this does not mean that we have to be the world's biggest bully. Our history has conditioned us to this, because, by and large, war has paid off for us. We are the only nation on earth that is not weary of war, that has had no disastrous experience in the last generation." Such is the temptation of abundance. Such is the temptation of having the marvelous extravagance of God visited upon us. The twelve baskets full left over become our temptation. What shall we do with them?

‡‡‡‡‡

JOHN 8:46-59

"ARE WE NOT RIGHT IN SAYING THAT YOU ARE A SAMARITAN AND HAVE A DEMON?"

"He who is of God hears the words of God; the reason you do not hear them is that you are not of God." [*John 8:47*] *The Jews were stuck on their vision of Abraham. They could not recognize Christ. "Are you greater than our Father Abraham?"* [*John 8:53*] *Jesus told the Jews off. "It is my Father who glorifies me of whom you say that He is your God, but you have not known him. I know him. If I said I do not know him I should be a liar like you."* [*John 8:54*]

The Jews kept the law, but they did not want the life. They preferred their prison of rules to the freedom of sonship Jesus offered. It seems safer in the box of our little religious habits than to venture everything on the Living God heart to heart.

Elizabeth Elliott wrote in the December Christian Herald.

One morning recently I read in the paper about a prisoner who had just been released after sixteen years and asked to remain in prison. He was denied the privilege, so down he went to a tavern, phoned the police to report a robbery and waited patiently until he was arrested as the thief. Back in his cell he explained that he felt at home there, that he wanted to finish an art course he had started in prison and that, furthermore, things had changed a lot in the outside world, and he didn't like it.

I wondered it he saw the cartoon that appeared in the New Yorker that same week, showing a guard complaining through the bars to a man in the striped outfit, saying, "Take me now. I'll go home on a packed bus, find the wife in tears over some crack a neighbor made, listen to a depressing newscast, bawl the kid out for a lousy report card, eat an underdone casserole, hassle over what TV show we're going to watch, find somebody else has taken the last beer in the icebox and finally settle into a fitful sleep punctured by a neighbor's hi-fi."

The prisoner in the cartoon is slumped down on a bench, hands clasped behind his head, listening to all of this and looking very pleased. People have different ideas of freedom, and they get out of one kind of freedom which order, security and sameness afford. Iron bars didn't bother him as much as change.

I understand that man. I don't like change very much. I am not always moving the furniture around. I don't want any "bright new taste surprises" for breakfast. I want the sofa where it was yesterday and the black coffee just the way I always make it.

Men will kill before they leave their Old Testament package life. It is so much easier to keep rules than it is to open your heart to God and let him take over; because we know exactly where we are with rules. We can keep them under control, but to let God keep us — to deliver ourselves to his wishes — we don't know where that will take us. We don't mind saying we won't steal, but saying we'll be God's friend is frightening.

So to stop Christ, the Jews condemned him: *"Are we not right in saying that you are a Samaritan and have a demon?"* [*John 8:48*] Demons were blamed for evil or madness in New Testament times. And if people didn't like something good you did, they could nail that as a demon. Several times Jesus was dismissed as having evil spirits.

But they had the demon, not Jesus. And demonology is not at all an obsolete interpretation of mental and moral illness. Derek Prince, a Cambridge educated Pentecostal, shows New Testament demonology compatible with modern psychoanalysis.

Demons are jealousy, hate, fear, lust and doubt that enter a good man and periodically control him. Prince believes that the Scriptures claim that any compulsion or addiction in a converted Christian that won't go away with prayer is a demon that must be cast out by another Christian in the Name of Christ.

He gives the example of two wives whose husbands have stopped loving them. One of these wives belongs to the Church of God and the other is an Episcopalian. The Church of God wife goes to the cookie jar for solace and the Episcopalian to the liquor cabinet. In the face of this frustration one becomes a compulsive eater, the other a compulsive drinker. Both are subject to these uncontrollable urges and are helpless without outside help.

When the victim can humble himself to ask for help and confess the problem to Christian friends, their prayers can brace his or her repentance and pull out the demon in the Name of the Lord Jesus Christ.

Casting out the demon involves the recollection of when it entered, as with Nicky Cruz's hatred. For instance, the demons of these Pharisees accusing Jesus certainly included doubt and pride, the worst demons of all. Here is an instance Prince relates of the exorcism of doubt from a student which also recalled its original entrance into him.

The student attended a meeting devoted to the deliverance from deeply rooted sins or demons. He vowed to leave the meeting exactly as he entered, but several hours later on a plane, his demon of doubt could be contained no longer. Years before when asked about Jesus' miracles he doubted Jesus could feed 5,000 people with five loaves and a few fishes and since that time doubt had held him prisoner from the faith. Now on this plane it seemed that the demon went out his ear, and since giving up a curse means unsaying what you said that started it off, he found himself turning to the complete stranger sitting next to him to announce: "I believe that Jesus Christ fed five thousand people with five loaves and a few fishes."

"Truly, truly I say to you, before Abraham was, I am." [*John 8:58*] Doubt will have to leave a man before he can make room for that. Those who cling tenaciously to their doubt and their pride will feel like doing as the Pharisees did then. *"So they took up stones to throw at Him, but Jesus hid Himself, and went out of the temple."* [*John 8:59*]

‡‡‡‡‡

JOHN 9:1-41

1. Blaming [*John 9:2*]

"Who sinned, this man or his parents?" the disciples asked. And Jesus replied, "Neither." But the disciples wanted to place blame on someone for this man's blindness. Why do so many people follow this practice? Often they hurt one another as they seek to find someone at whom they can point the finger of accusation. After all, none of us is blameless. Scriptures tell us "all have sinned." It is sometimes a case of self-righteousness when we try to lay blame on someone. By doing so we disrupt human relations. Even nations have been artful in this practice, going to war on the basis of first laying blame on the enemy. Colleges blame high schools for the defects of their students; high schools blame the grade schools, while grade schools blame the parents and homes. Rather than follow such a practice we need to look at ourselves, asking what God will find when he probes into our life. Also, it is time to stop passing the buck and to get at the work of making necessary improvements. Helping, not blaming, must be the order of the day.

2. Christ is a prophet [*John 9:17*]

The Greek word used here is *prophetes.* It has basically two meanings. One is foreteller, revealing future events that are to take place under the hand of God. Divine inspiration is implied, contact with the Almighty. The other meaning is forthtelling, explaining the Scriptures, having divine inspiration which leads to exhortation, and sometimes reproof. Giving guidance to individuals and to nations as God's interpreter and his ambassador. Thus Jesus as prophet is the foremost example or revealer of God's love, making clear God's plan of redemption for all mankind.

3. I believe [*John 9:38*]

Children in church school sing "Jesus loves me, this I know, for the Bible tells me so." To retain this simple belief all through life is the kernel of Christian faith. Jesus said "unless we have faith as a little child" we will not enter into the kingdom. In a sense we always remain "children" of the heavenly father. One time the world-renowned theologian Karl Barth was asked what he would consider the greatest truth he had discovered in all his reading and thinking. His astonishingly simple reply was, "The greatest truth I have ever learned is 'Jesus loves me.' " In childhood and in the wisdom of maturity this is the great essential of Christian faith.

Like the man healed of blindness we must "see" that Jesus, who revealed the power of God, loves us, and say to Christ, "Lord, I believe.

4. Are we blind also? [*John 9:40*]

What a question to ask ourselves. The answer might surprise us. How much of God do we see? He is all about us. A great scientist went home to lunch after spending the morning in his laboratory peering through a powerful microscope at the petals of a rose. When his wife asked him how he had been spending his time he replied, "I have spent the morning with God." It was Oliver St. John Gogarty who wrote:

What can we say but, "Glory be,"
When God bursts out in an apple tree?

Do we see God in nature, in humanity? Or are we blind also?

‡‡‡‡‡

JOHN 11:1-53

1. God moves slowly [*John 11:6*]

When Jesus heard of the death of his good friend Lazarus, it saddened him but he did not go immediately to Bethany to restore his friend to life. Rather, he "stayed where he was for the next two days and made no move to go." How often we get impatient with one another, which is not good. But far worse still is to get impatient with God, as though he were at our beck and call. We cannot expect immediate answers to prayer. God takes his time. The world was millions of years in creation. The old axiom states that "the mills of the gods grind slowly, but they grind exceedingly fine." God often moves slowly in stark contrast to the feverish activity of little mortals. Perhaps he delays an answer to our prayer to test us, to see whether we really desire what we are requesting, or whether we have sufficient confidence that he hears. We want what we want when we want it. But a wise man has said that life is "a song of degrees"; it is a ladder, up which we must climb step by step. When we try to force things we often lose them. So Jesus first completed his work where he was, and then went to raise Lazarus. The important thing is that in the right time he did respond. We must measure life not only by our watch, but by God's great time clock.

2. How great is your faith? [*John 11:22*]

When Christ came to Bethany, following the death of Lazarus, the body had been in the tomb long enough for decay to set in. For Christ to be expected to restore the body to life now took even more faith than it would if he had been present immediately after Lazarus' death. But still Mary's faith in Christ was unwavering. She told Christ that she knew that "even now" he could perform the miracle of restoring her brother from death.

We tend to limit our faith. We think that some things can be accomplished by prayer, or through Christ, but how much? We fail to comprehend how great God is, or to realize the limitless height and depth and width of Christ's love. *Your God Is Too Small* is the catching title of a book. It could well be paraphrased to read, "Your Faith Is Too Small." It is never too late to expect miracles of Jesus. In old age as well as youth, no matter how late in the game, the addiction to dope or liquor or some mortal sin, "even now" Christ can come to the rescue if we put our faith in him.

3. When Christ calls [*John 11:28*]

In the King James version the text reads: "The Master has come, and calleth for you." This has been used as a funeral text, reminding the mourners that death for a Christian is simply the call of Christ to come up higher, that he who is the resurrection and the life is leading a loved one into the fulfillment of highest hopes. But Christ calls all through life, not just at death. He calls us to Christian service and to a life of faith.

Charles Lamb once made an interesting observation: "Not many sounds in life, and I include all urban and rural sounds, exceed in interest a knock at the door." It is true, for a sense of curiosity and of expectancy rises quickly in our emotional response to the sound of a knock. Christ is continually knocking and we must hear him as he seeks in many ways to attract our attention. His knock on the door of our life is the most important of all. When it sounds, do we pretend not to have heard or that we are not at home? We will have to answer his knock if we are to have fellowship with him and receive the blessings he has come to bestow.

‡‡‡‡‡

JOHN 20:1-9

1. She ran! [*John 20:2*]

There are so many lethargic Christians. Their religion doesn't move them. They like to practice "armchair religion," where they sit and are enlightened by the preacher of the Gospel, but they don't want to leave the comfort of their chairs. It has been said that there are millions of Christians who would be embarrassed to get excited about it. Such excitement, they think, is not proper decorum. Hence, in their many daily contacts, no one even knows they are Christians. In heaven's name, what should excite us more? The love of God has been shed upon us. "Now we are children of God." Christ is "with us always." "All things are yours." "Whatsoever ye shall ask in Christ's name ye shall receive." If these earth-shaking pronouncements don't rouse us, nothing can. With Mary it was different. She ran! She was so excited about the news that Christ had risen. And as for us, the hour is late. We too should run to proclaim Christ to our neighbor, to finish God's tasks assigned to us, to exult in the death of death and to enter into the newness of life with our resurrected Lord.

2. Then I saw and believed [*John 20:8*]

Jesus said of one of his disciples that he believed in the resurrection because he had touched the wounded hands and side of Christ after he arose from the tomb. And Christ added that more blessed are folks like we who have not seen and yet believe. But why would we not believe? Surely the God who created heaven and earth and gave us life in the first place can give us life again, as he has promised to do.

Once Queen Victoria visited a paper mill where she was shown a room filled with filthy rags and pieces of carpet, out of which paper was to be made. She wondered aloud how such things would ever produce pure white paper. She was told that chemicals would make it possible to produce highest quality bond paper. Later the factory owner sent her a package of the same as an example. But he had the temerity to enclose an old saying that God could do the same thing for a Christian by removing all the stains and dirt of sin. Though we have not seen the resurrected Lord, he *has* risen and we must believe it and need to be like the woman described on a tombstone:

Here lies one doubly blest:
She was happy, and she knew it.

Christ saves us, cleanses us, will raise us up after death. Believe it!

3. We hadn't realized that the Scriptures said . . . [*John 20:9*]

How much do we know what the Scriptures say? In a day of Biblical illiteracy people seem to know less and less of the glorious things on those pages of holy writ. But they are there for us to read, and to realize that they apply to us. It is God's personal message for each of us.

A most interesting incident is told concerning a Chinese man whose first name was Lo. When he became a convert to Christianity and read the Bible he became greatly excited when he read his name in various places, such as "Lo I am with you always." He thought the message was to him, personally. And he was right! The Scriptures are for our edification. Their promises apply to us. We can insert our own name in all of the glorious promises, for they are meant for us. It is of us that the Bible says, "Though he were dead, yet shall he live." O wonderful Easter message of everlasting life — for us.

‡‡‡‡‡

1 CORINTHIANS 5:7-8

"Cleanse out the old leaven that you may be a new lump." [*Cor. 5:7*] *Leaven is sin. Get rid of it. This is a lifelong task.*

In a luncheon address at Anaheim, California, Mrs. Billy Graham emphasized the point that each life is a continuous process of learning. "If I had to select words to be inscribed on my tombstone," she said, "I would borrow these from a road sign: 'End of Construction. Thank You for Your Patience.' "

"For Christ, our Paschal Lamb, has been sacrificed." (1 Cor. 5:7). This enables us to make the change. The Cross was the Enabling Act of man's redemption — not an act passed by Congress, but an act of God, a rescue that closed the gap between the two worlds of what we are and what we ought.

"Let us, therefore, celebrate the festival, not with the old leaven, the leaven of malice and evil, but with the unleavened bread of sincerity and truth." (1 Cor. 5:8)

"The truth will set you free." Freud unwittingly founded psychoanalysis on that verse. If you get in touch with yourself — what pulls, pushes or bugs you — you are entering the new world a free man.

What a man doesn't know does, too, hurt him. The devil is an imposter, the one who tells lies. His most distinguishing characteristic is his insincerity. Lies and violence go together. They build scaffolds and prisons.

Hell is a triumph of deceit, and the new leaven is able to seek and celebrate the truth sincerely.

A couple I know made a New Year's resolution to be completely honest in their social life. "It all began with a friend calling every Monday morning to make plans with us for the following weekend," the wife explained. "I'd say okay – whether we wanted to see them or not – because I could never come up with a quick excuse. Then my husband and I would spend all week trying to figure out a way to cancel. We finally realized that it is all right to refuse any invitation."

A friend of mine recently underwent the chores of moving. As the movers were gathering their barrels and boxes, she realized that she hadn't seen a valuable vase. Carefully, the four men went through every barrel of excelsior, every box of papers, while my friend and her young daughter searched closets and cupboard shelves. After an hour, on the verge of giving up, the woman's eyes caught the gleam of crystal on the kitchen floor. The girl looked at her mother and burst into tears. "I dropped it early this morning," she confessed. My friend was distressed over the loss of a treasure, naturally. But she was more distressed over the unnecessary trouble her child had caused. "You have wasted an hour for six people," she pointed out. "That's six hours – almost a day's work." The girl wiped her eyes. "But I think I learned a lesson, Mother," she said. [*"A Simple Shortcut That Will Set You Free," Elise Miller Davis, Reader's Digest*]

The truth is that we are going to die. Face it honestly. Only that can prepare us to face the truth of the resurrection. And, of course, that truth is reached only by following him who said, "I am the Truth." The devil is the one who plays us false; Christ is honest. This is something to get uproariously happy about. Liberation from the prison of pretense that we have so long wrapped ourselves in.

‡‡‡‡‡

1 CORINTHIANS 5:7, 8

"CLEANSE OUT THE OLD LEAVEN THAT YOU MAY BE A NEW LUMP"

I suppose that the oldest controversy in history is the struggle between the old and the new. Even our Lord got into it one day when he said to the religious leaders: "No one puts a new patch on an old garment" . . . and . . . "neither is new wine put into old wine skins." So the conflict goes on between the past and the future. In age after age, there are patchers and there are creators — some who try to patch up the thread-bare garment, and some who are forever trying to create a new and a better one. Where do Christians belong in the argument? In a time of radical change, where do the followers of Christ stand? This is no longer just an academic question. We have to face it now and make up our minds about it. The biographers of King Louis XVI said of him: "He was an amiable and upright man who would doubtless have made a good leader in a time of peace." Unfortunately, his ancestors had bequeathed Louis the XVI a revolution, and that is where we are, too. We have inherited a revolution, and we shall live out our days where the old and the new are clashing furiously. We carry in our own hearts the conflict that is raging without let-up throughout the world. David Rockefeller, when he was elected the "Businessman of the Year," said what so many others have said in many other ways: "In life today the past is being overwhelmed by the future. There has been a transformation so swift in pace and so profound in social implications that it has outstripped the perception of most historians." What is a Christian? I see nothing wrong with Paul's description: "If any man be in Christ, he is a new creature. Old things are passed away. Behold, all things are become new." One of the oddest things imaginable is a Christian allergic to change, when he himself is a product of The Changer, or a Christian afraid of the new, when he himself has been made new. A patched coat is not a good symbol of a Christian. He may sometimes have to wear one, but he was never meant to be one. The key word in the New Testament is "new."

All progress is made by the simple technique of building in the present on some foundation of the past, taking the gains of yesterday and going further with them today. A good observation has been made on this. It takes two hands to make a clock tell time. One hand goes fast and one goes slowly, and it takes both hands to make a good clock. Perhaps it takes both to make a good country or a good church. Stanley Jones once said that if we were all liberal, we would blow up; if we were all conservative, we would dry up. It has never been better said than by Winston Churchill: "If we open a quarrel between the past and the present, we shall find that we have lost the future."

*****

The New Testament is not a conservative book. We cannot stop with the old. That is what makes revolutions. Custom! How many rivers grow stagnant in that swamp? How many garments have been torn on that old nail? Custom! The way we have always done it, the things we keep on doing, the words we keep on saying after the light has gone out of them or leaped ahead of them. For instance, examine the sleeve of a man's coat. There are two buttons there, or three buttons, or maybe four buttons. There is absolutely no need for those buttons. Custom put them there. We are told that in the monasteries the old monks with loose robes had trouble eating their soup, so they sewed buttons on their sleeves to keep their sleeves out of the soup. We no longer wear the robes, but we still have the buttons. We have all sorts of buttons brought over from yesterday, all sorts of things that we do not need, customs we have outgrown, habits of thought grown stuffy and musty with the years. Most of us have lived in towns where someplace in town there was a cattle path through a pasture, which had become a footpath for men, and then a wagon track, and then a road, and then an improved road and finally a city street. We wonder who could have laid out such a crooked, meandering street, and we never face the fact that we are following the path of some stupid, wandering cow.

‡‡‡‡‡

"BUT EMPTIED HIMSELF, TAKING ON THE FORM OF A SERVANT . . . AND BEING FOUND IN HUMAN FORM, HE HUMBLED HIMSELF."

What would you include in a list of Christian virtues today? Ben Franklin wrote a list of twelve, and he forgot humility. Socrates said that there was only one really essential virtue and that was wisdom. The ancient philosophers who followed Socrates listed four cardinal virtues: wisdom, courage, temperance, and justice. But make no mistake about it, dear friends, Christian ethics goes much higher and much deeper than that. They are more sensitive and they are more social. Too many people, even today, live their lives on the level of pagan morality. Pagan ethics was most concerned about a man's relationship to himself. "Know thyself," said the ancient philosophers.

Christian ethics, on the other hand, have to do with man's relationship to God and with his fellow man. So when wise old Paul writes to his young friend, Timothy, he makes a list of six virtues: righteousness, Godliness, faith, love, patience. These five, I am sure, most of us would include in a list of Christian virtues, but the last one is the puzzler, foreign to everything we believe and think in our day. The last is "meekness" — meekness! Look! Have you ever heard anyone in our day who is congratulated or lauded or applauded or admired because of his meekness? We seldom have the chance. In fact, there is something repugnant to us about the whole idea of meekness. Use the word "meek" and we immediately conjure up a vision of a kind of Mr. Milquetoast. Think of the analogies that we use: "Meek as a mouse" — a shy, frightened, scurrying little soul, flitting around the edges of life trying to keep out of everybody's way. "Meek as a lamb," we say. Well, lambs may be lovable, but we pity them for their stupid helplessness. We certainly don't admire their spirit. Everything about meekness runs completely counter to our ideas of what makes for a happy and successful life.

*****

Probably the most demanding, meticulous job in the City of Washington, D.C. today is the Chief of Protocol. Among his tasks is placing people in their rank at State dinners, and Heaven help the poor man if he should make a mistake. Recently a special microphone, we are told, was installed on the outside of the President's bullet-proof, sound-proof limousine, so they can hear within the car the cheers of the multitude that go on outside the limousine, which, I suspect, is a far cry from Thomas Jefferson, who rode his own horse alone to his own inauguration. Our Lord says: *"The first shall be last and the last first,"* and we don't believe a word of it. To us, that's a blatant lie. We take our philosophy from men like Leo Durocher, who says: "Nice guys always end up in last place." St. Augustine said that there were three important Christian virtues. The first is humility; the second is humility, the third is humility.

*****

Mary Wells, who is the head of a highly successful and rapidly growing advertising agency on Madison Avenue, New York, says of her fast rise to power and popularity and wealth: "This is our moment, and I'm not the least bit humble about it." The motto of the firm is: "If we were only modest, we'd be perfect." It was the late Fred Allen who was called as a witness before a Congressional Investigating Committee, and in the course of the questioning, as was the custom, he was asked what he did for a living. He said: "I'm the world's greatest comedian." His family, later on, asked him why in the world he made such a conceited statement in public. He said: "Well, ordinarily, I wouldn't have, but, you see, I was under oath." Or they tell of a man who went to a psychiatrist, and someone asked him how it had helped him. He replied: "Well, before I went, I was egotistical, conceited and unbearable to people. I didn't have any friends. Nobody liked me. But now, I'm the most likable, modest, humble guy you ever met, and everybody loves me."

‡‡‡‡‡

PHILIPPIANS 2:5-11

1. A right attitude [*Philippians 2:5*]

We are asked to have the attitude of Christ, which means to think as he did and to make judgments similar to his. This means, furthermore, that we must bring our thoughts under Christ's influence. The Negro spiritual sings out "Lord, I want to be a Christian in my heart." We need to sing also: Lord, I want to be a Christian in my head. The commandment exhorts us to love the Lord with all our mind. The first step in securing the mind of Christ is to read his gospels, to learn what he thought and taught. The second step is to let his thoughts influence our thinking. The illustration has been used of a lunch box, carried to work. Through the morning the owner would look at it and anticipate enjoying its contents. But when noon came the food was consumed and then, inside of him it provided energy and health. The Gospels are not just to be looked at or read. It is when the truth gets into our minds to control our thoughts and actions that the truth takes effect.

2. Christ is the example of humility [*Philippians 2:8*]

Humility is a virtue, but we do not come by it easily. Human nature has to fight a selfish ego that craves the number one spot. Paul describes the humility of Christ who was willing to leave his place in heaven to be subjected to the humiliation and suffering of death upon a cross. St. Paul says this act of Christ's was an example for all of us, that we should not be arrogant nor think of ourselves more highly than we ought to think.

The great preacher, John Henry Jowett, was jolted one time by a prayer offered on his behalf, but he acknowledged its propriety. He was conducting a religious service and the man who was to offer prayer uttered these words: "O Lord, we thank thee for our dear brother. Now by the grace of God blot him out that we may see Jesus only." Jowett had great fame. Many came to the service to hear him. But the need of the people was not to see Jowett given further acclaim; their need was to be inspired by Christ. We must be humble enough that no conduct or arrogance can crowd Christ from our life or obscure him from others. Our model is Christ himself, who "though he was the Son of God, humbled Himself and became obedient even unto death on the cross."

3. Christ will be honored [*Philippians 2:10, 11*]

One of the most thrilling statements of the New Testament is that which declares that "at the name of Jesus every knee shall bow . . . and every tongue declare that He is Lord." This thought brings to mind the tens of thousands of the faithful who gather from all over the world outside St. Peter's in Rome to do Christ honor. Or one thinks of the great gatherings where over 100,000 honor Christ as Lord at a service conducted by Billy Graham. Perhaps most thrilling of all was when the mighty empress, Queen Victoria, sat on her throne, listening to the performance of the Hallelujah Chorus by a great choir. As the words poured forth from many throats, "and He shall reign for ever and ever," Queen Victoria rose from her throne and removed her crown. Nothing on this earth can prevent the arrival of that day when Christ will be elevated in the eyes of all mankind to his rightful position of "King of kings and Lord of lords."

Worship Resources

Special Services for Lent and Easter Ralph E. Dessem

THE SERVICE OF WORSHIP

Prelude
Hymn of Praise
Call to Worship

Minister: God so loved the world that he gave his only Son, that whoever believes in him should not perish but have eternal life.

People: Christ also died for sins once for all, the righteous and the unrighteous, that he might bring us to God.

Minister: God did not spare his own Son but gave him up for us all.

People: Greater love has no man than this, that a man lay down his life for his friends.

Collect

Father of all, in all our ways of life we seek your help; in all our perplexities of thought, your counsel; in all our dangers of temptation, your protection; and in all our sorrows of heart, your peace; Grant, O Father, that as we move in the world of men they may sense that we seek to follow the example of Jesus of Nazareth, in whose name we pray. Amen.

Gloria Patri
Prayer of Confession

Gracious Father, we come before you as a rebellious and sinful people. We have disobeyed your commandments; we have worshiped ourselves and the things we have made. We have rejected your will for our lives; we have preferred our way to that of Christ. Forgive us, O Lord, for straying away from that which you intended for us to be, and for failing to follow the example of Christ. Amen.

Assurance of Pardon

Lord's Prayer

Choral Selection

Scripture Reading

Affirmation of Faith (in unison)

We believe in God, the Eternal Spirit, Father of our Lord Jesus Christ and our Father, and to his deeds we testify:

He calls the worlds into being,
creates man in his own image
and sets before him the ways of life and death.
He seeks in holy love to save all people from aimlessness and sin.
He judges men and nations by his righteous will declared through prophets and apostles.

In Jesus Christ, the man of Nazareth, our crucified and risen Lord,
He has come to us and shared our common lot,
conquering sin and death
and reconciling the world to himself.

He bestows upon us his Holy Spirit,
creating and renewing the Church of Jesus Christ,
binding in covenant faithful people of all ages, tongues and races.

He calls us into his Church
to accept the cost and joy of discipleship,
to be his servants in the service of men,
to proclaim the gospel to all the world
and resist the powers of evil,
to share in Christ's Baptism and eat at his table,
to join him in his passion and victory.

He promises to all who trust him
forgiveness of sins and fullness of grace,
courage in the struggle for justice and peace,
his presence in trial and rejoicing,
and eternal life in his kingdom which has no end.

Blessing and honor, glory and power be unto Him. Amen.

Pastoral Prayer
Hymn of Adoration
Presentation of Offerings
Doxology
Sermon
Words of Dedication

Minister: You have heard the message of God given through Christ, and through me. Will you now seek to apply these words in your own Christian living?

People: We will accept this as our Christian obligation and responsibility.

Minister: God will bless you and guide you as you witness to him.

People: We will go forth with his blessing.

Hymn of Dedication
Benediction
Postlude

‡‡‡‡‡

THE SERVICE OF WORSHIP

The Prelude
The Hymn of Praise
The Call to Worship

Minister: The Lord is merciful and gracious, slow to anger and abounding in steadfast love.

People: He does not deal with us according to our sins, nor requite us according to our iniquities.

Minister: What shall I render to the Lord for all his benefits toward me?

People: I will lift up the cup of salvation and call on the name of the Lord.

The Collect

Eternal God, You are in our midst and are always ready to hear our prayers. You already know our innermost longings and are aware of our needs. Our perpetual need is for your mercy and love. Though we are most unworthy, we reach for your forgiving love and claim anew Your gracious acceptance, through Jesus Christ our Lord. Amen.

The Gloria Patri

The Prayer of Confession (in unison)

Most merciful Father, we know that we have failed to follow your guidance, and have failed to do your will. We have allowed self to blind us, pains to embitter us, and trials to discourage us. While we are mindful of the love of Christ for us, we have failed to deny ourselves so that we might follow him completely. Pardon our shortcomings; forgive our neglect; give us a pure heart intent on following and pleasing you; in the name of Christ. Amen.

The Assurance of Pardon

The Lord's Prayer

The Choral Selection

The Scripture Lesson [*Read responsively*] *Luke 9:18-26*

Minister: As he was praying alone the disciples were with him; and he asked them, "Who do the people say that I am?"

People: *And they answered, "John the Baptist; but others say, Elijah; and others, that one of the old prophets has risen."*

Minister: And he said to them, "But who do you say that I am?"

People: *And Peter answered, "The Christ of God."*

Minister: But he charged and commanded them to tell this to no one, saying, "The Son of man must suffer many things, and be rejected by the elders and chief priests and scribes, and be killed, and on the third day be raised."

People: *And he said to all, "If any man would come after me, let him deny himself and take up his cross daily and follow me.*

Minister: For whoever would save his life will lose it; and whoever loses his life for my sake, he will save it.

People: *For what does it profit a man if he gains the whole world and loses or forfeits himself?*

All: *For whoever is ashamed of me and of my words, of him will the Son of man be ashamed when He comes in His glory."*

The Pastoral Prayer

The Hymn of Devotion

The Presentation of Offerings

The Doxology

The Sermon

The Prayer of Dedication

Our Father, we realize people are not crucified upon crosses today. Though we face none made of wood, we know there are causes that are like crosses which demand total sacrifice.

Point us toward the cross of decision where we single out our loyalties and define objectives so that we know our life purpose.

Guide us toward the cross of justice so that we can interpret the issues clustering around great decisions.

Direct us toward the cross of service so that our personalities will grow with exercise, our talents increase by use, and our resources develop by exposure to the generosity of living.

Help us sacrifice the petty pleasures, the idle hours, the wasted energies, the misguided dreams, the worthless trinkets, and senseless goals.

Make our sacrifices and crosses count in the divine plan of love. Amen.

The Hymn of Dedication

The Benediction

The Postlude

‡‡‡‡‡

THE SERVICE OF WORSHIP

Prelude
Hymn of Praise
Call to Worship

Minister: Greetings in the name of Jesus Christ.
People: We greet you in the name of the Father Almighty.
Minister: We gather together to allow the Holy Spirit to speak to us, to inspire us and to challenge us.
People: Let us worship together that we might receive these spiritual benefits.

Collect

Almighty God, we praise and glorify you as Father, Son and Holy Spirit. Grant that in the majesty of your creation we may realize your power, that in the life of Jesus Christ we may receive your love that seeks and saves us, and that in the presence of the Holy Spirit we may experience the newness of your life within. Reveal yourself to us, in all of your fulness, O gracious Triune God. Amen.

Glori Patri
Prayer of Confession (in unison)

O Lord, be merciful to us in the midst of our sins and transgressions. We have not loved you with our whole heart. We have rejected your way of life as revealed through Jesus Christ. We have failed to permit your Holy Spirit to guide us in all things. We have not loved our neighbors and ourselves. We have been conformed to the material world around us, rather than allowing your Spirit to transform us into the persons that we ought to be; forgive us, we pray through Christ. Amen.

Assurance of Pardon
Lord's Prayer
Scripture Reading
Choral Selection

Call to Prayer (may be read in unison by two groups in congregation)

Creator of the stars of night
Our people's everlasting light,
O Christ, the Saviour of us all,
We praise You, hear us when we call
At the holy name of Jesus, now
All knees must bend, all hearts must bow;
And things celestial Yours shall be,
And things terrestrial, Lord alone.
Come in Your holy might, we pray;
Redeem us for eternal day
From every power of darkness when
You shall judge all the sons of men.
To God the Father, God the Son
And God the Spirit, Three in One.
Laud, honor might and glory be
From age to age eternally.

(9th Century Latin Hymn)

Pastoral Prayer
Hymn of Adoration
Presentation of Offerings
Doxology
Sermon
Litany of Reflection

Minister: Do you now consider yourselves Christians?
People: Yes, but we follow sometimes timidly.
Minister: Without conviction, without power,
People: We often forget, and we neglect,
Minister: And sometimes we downright ignore God.
People: Good Lord, forgive us!
Minister: Christ, have mercy on us!
People: Holy Spirit, renew us!

Prayer of Dedication
Hymn of Faith
Benediction
Postlude

THE TENEBRAE SERVICE

(The service of Tenebrae follows a tradition of the church dating back to at least the 8th and perhaps as early as the 5th century. It dramatizes the suffering, death, and burial of Jesus Christ. The service moves from light to darkness, with the diminishing light symbolizing the fading devotion of the apostles. It is hoped that each person present will become more aware of the sadness and despair that were evident before and during the crucifixion. At the end of the service the sanctuary will be in darkness with the exception of the exit lights. There will be no benediction; each person is asked to leave silently as he contemplates th tragedy of the crucifixion. Jesus, the Son of God, is dead; there is nothing more to do but wait — for the day of Resurrection!)

The Prelude

The Light of the World

The Call to Worship

Minister: Jesus said, I am the light of the world. Whoever follows me will have the light of life and will never walk in darkness.

People: This was the real light, the light that comes into the world and shines on all men.

Minister: If we live in the light — just as he is in the light — then we have fellowship with one another.

People: The darkness is passing away, and the real light is already shining.

The Hymn of Illumination

The Invocation

The Gathering of the Apostles

The Scripture Reading *Matthew 4:18-22*

The Testimony of the Apostles

(As each apostle introduces himself, he lights a candle which symbolizes his relationship with Jesus, the Christ.)

Peter	Philip
John	Thomas
Judas Iscariot	James
James, son of Alphaeus	Bartholomew
Andrew	Simon the Zealot
Matthew	Thaddaeus

The Hymn of Devotion

The Task of the Apostles

The Scripture Reading

Minister: What did Jesus charge you to do as apostles?

Apostles: To go and preach; "The Kingdom of heaven is near." He also charged us to heal the sick, raise the dead, and make the lepers clean, and drive out demons." [Matthew 10:7, 8]

Minister: What is the cost of discipleship?

Apostles: Jesus said, "Listen! I am sending you just like sheep to a pack of wolves. You must be as cautious as snakes and as gentle as doves. Watch out, for there will be men who will arrest you and take you to court, and they will whip you in their synagogues. You will be brought to trial before rulers and kings for my sake, to tell the Good News to them and to the Gentiles. When they bring you to trial, do not worry about what you will say or how you will say it; when the times comes, you will be given what you will say. For the words you speak will not be yours; they will come from the Spirit of your Father speaking in you. [Matthew 10:16-20]

The Hymn of Discipleship

The Time of Testing

The Scripture Reading *Matthew 26:1-4, 31-35*

The Departure of the Apostles

Minister: Then all the apostles left him and ran away. (Apostles extinguish their candles and depart.)
With only the light of the Christ candle remaining, we contemplate the loneliness of our Saviour.

The Solo "Were You There When They Crucified my Lord?"

The Voice of the Prophet *Isaiah 53:3-9*

The Period of Contemplation

Minister: With only the glimmer of the Christ candle, we sit in semi-darkness and contemplate God's love for us as seen in Christ on the cross.

[*People will respond with brief prayers given audibly and spontaneously.*]

The Death of the Christ

The Extinguishing of the Christ Candle

The Moments of Meditation

The Departure in Silence

"Christ is dead! We await his Resurrection!"

‡‡‡‡‡

THE SERVICE OF TENEBRAE

(Our service is an adaptation of the ancient Tenebrae service, dating from the 8th century. It is a service of worship that moves from light to darkness with the fading light symbolizing the fading loyalty of the disciples and friends of Jesus. During the reading of the Scripture portions that appear on the bulletin, the crowd will be portrayed by the congregation.)

Prelude

Words of Praise — *Mark 11:1, 4, 7-10*

Narrator: And then they drew near to Jerusalem, at the mount of Olives, he sent two of his disciples. And they went away, and found a colt tied and they untied it. And they brought the colt to Jesus and threw their clothes on it; and he sat upon it. And many spread their clothes on the road and others spread leafy branches which they had cut from the fields. And those who went before and those who followed cried out:

People: *Hosanna! Blessed be he who comes in the name of the Lord! Blessed be the kingdom of our father David that is coming. Hosanna in the highest!*

Hymn of Triumph

"All Glory, Laud and Honor" (St. Theodulph)

Invocation

Almighty God, our Father, help us to be mindful of those events that occurred in the life of Jesus during that last week in Jerusalem. As we become aware of the manner in which the disciples, the members of the crowd, and others failed him, we pray that you will quicken our hearts that we might not be guilty of the same sins today. Forgive us for those occasions when we have failed to exert a strong witness for you, and so guide through Jesus Christ our Lord. Amen.

THE DARKNESS OF MISUNDERSTANDING

Words in the Temple — *Mark 11:15-18*
John 10:28-36

Narrator: And He entered the temple and began to drive out those who sold and those who bought in the temple. And He taught and said to them:

Jesus: Is it not written, "My house shall be called a house of prayer for all nations? But you have made it a den of robbers."

Narrator: And the chief priests and scribes heard it and sought a way to destroy him; for they feared him, because all the multitude was astonished at his teaching. Then a voice came from heaven. The crowd standing by heard it and said that it had thundered. Jesus answered:

Jesus: This voice has come for your sake, not for mine. Now shall the ruler of this world be cast out; and I, when I am lifted up from the earth, will draw all men to myself.

Narrator: He said this to show what death he was to die. The crowd answered him:

People: We have heard from the law that the Christ remains forever. How can you say that the Son of man must be lifted up? Who is the Son of man?

Jesus: The light is with you a little longer. Walk while you have the light, lest the darkness overtake you; he who walks in the darkness does not know where he goes. While you have the light, believe in the light, that you may become sons of light.

[*The first candle is extinguished*]

Choir Anthem

THE DARKNESS OF BETRAYAL

Words in the Upper Room — *Matthew 26:20-28*

[*The second candle is extinguished.*]

Hymn of Devotion

THE DARKNESS OF TEMPTATION

Words in the Garden — *Matthew 26:30-31, 36-46*

[*The third candle is extinguished.*]

Hymn of Faithfulness

THE DARKNESS OF INJUSTICE

Words of the Trial — *Mark 14:53, 57-64; 15:1-5*
Luke 23:7, 11

[*The fourth candle is extinguished.*]

Hymn of Sorrow

THE DARKNESS OF DENIAL

Words of the Courtyard — *Mark 14:66-72*

[*The fifth candle is extinguished.*]

Hymn of Intercession

THE DARKNESS OF REJECTION

Words Before Pilate — *Luke 23:13-24*

Narrator: Pilate then called together the chief priests and the rulers of the people, and said to them:

Pilate: You brought me this man as one who was perverting the people; and after examining him before you, behold, I did not find this man guilty of any of your charges against him; neither did Herod, for he sent him back to us. Behold, nothing deserving death has been done by him; I will therefore chastise him and release him.

Narrator: But they all cried out together:

People: Crucify, crucify him!

Pilate: Why, what evil has he done? I have found in him no crime deserving of death; I will therefore chastise him and release him.

Narrator: But they were urgent, demanding with loud cries that he should be crucified:

People: Crucify him! Crucify him!

Narrator: And their voices prevailed. So Pilate gave sentence that their demands should be granted.

[*The sixth candle is extinguished.*]

Hymn of Penitence

THE DARKNESS OF CRUCIFIXION

Words on the Cross *Luke 23:33-34; 39-43*
John 19:26-30
Matthew 27:45-46
Luke 23:46-48

[*The seventh candle is extinguished*]

Solo "Were You There When They Crucified My Lord?"

Benediction

[*The congregation will leave quietly in semi-darkness.*]

Postlude

‡‡‡‡‡

THE SERVICE OF WORSHIP
THE SEVEN LAST WORDS

The Prelude

The Call to Worship

Minister: God so loved the world that he gave his only Son, that whosoever believes in him should not perish but have eternal life.

People: God did not spare his own Son, but gave him up for us all.

Minister: Christ also died for sins once for all, the righteous for the unrighteous, that he might bring us to God.

People: Behold, the Lamb of God, who takes away the sin of the world!

The Invocation (in unison)

Almighty God, our Father, in this period of meditation and prayer may our attention be focused on him who gave his life for us and who revealed to us the greatness of your love. We pray that you will so guide us during our worship together that we might receive a new sense of appreciation for that which he did for us as he gave his life upon the cross, through Jesus Christ our Lord. Amen.

THE WORDS OF FORGIVENESS . . . Love Intercedes
"Father, forgive them for they know not what they do."

The Scripture Reading *Luke 23:24-34*
The Meditation on the First Word
The Prayer

O most merciful God, we are mindful of our sinfulness. You know that we have sinned against you, as well as against others, and have failed to follow the example of your Son. Grant us your forgiveness as we would be willing to forgive others, in the name of Jesus Christ our Savior. Amen.

The Hymn
The Silent Prayer and Meditation

THE WORD OF PARDON . . . Love Rescues
"Today you will be with me in Paradise."

The Anthem
The Scripture Reading *Luke 23:35-43*
The Meditation on the Second Word
The Prayer

Infinite and eternal God, we call upon you in the spirit of penitence. You have granted us the gifts and benefits of life in a greater way than we deserve. Many times we have taken these benefits for granted and have failed to express our appreciation for them. Pardon us for what we have been, and direct what we shall be, through Christ our Lord. Amen.

The Hymn
The Silent Prayer and Meditation

THE WORD OF CONCERN . . .
Love Creates Community
"Woman, behold your son . . . Behold your mother."

The Scripture Reading *John 19:23-27*
The Meditation on the Third Word
The Prayer

O God of Love, let us not forget the greatness of love as shown forth in your Son. As we are mindful of his suffering upon the cross, help us to realize anew that in this experience he expressed his love and concern for others — his enemies as well as his loved ones. Guide us as we would seek to express our love each day, in the Savior's name. Amen.

The Hymn

The Silent Prayer and Meditation

THE WORD OF LONELINESS . . . Love Obeys God

"My God! My God! Why hast thou forsaken me?"

The Anthem

The Scripture Reading *Mark 15:29-34*

The Meditation on the Fourth Word

The Prayer

Our Heavenly Father, forgive us when we feel that we are completely forgotten. With the unseen presence of the Christ dwelling within our hearts, we are never really alone but are bound to you with a spiritual kinship. Sustain us from within and inspire us to seek to live in spiritual companionship with you, through Jesus Christ our Lord. Amen.

The Hymn

The Silent Prayer and Meditation

THE WORD OF SUFFERING . . .
Love Bears Punishment

"I thirst."

The Scripture Reading *John 19:28-29*

The Meditation on the Fifth Word

The Prayer

Almighty God, we know that your son suffered in more ways that we can ever realize. His agony on the cross was merely the culmination of a life of pain, misery, desertion, ridicule, and criticism. Might we ever remember that it was for us that he was willing to endure all these things. Help us also to understand that he can inspire us in the midst of our suffering and tribulation, through our Lord Jesus Christ. Amen.

The Hymn

The Silent Prayer and Meditation

THE WORD OF VICTORY . . . Love Offers Sacrifice
"It is finished."

The Anthem
The Scripture Reading *John 19:30-37*
The Meditation on the Sixth Word
The Prayer

Everlasting God, let us never forget that you are the great Supreme Being of the universe. Even though we sometimes feel that the spirit of evil is winning in the battle of life, may be ever be mindful of the fact that the spirit of Divine Truth will achieve the final victory, through him who is the Way, the Truth, and the Life. Amen.

The Hymn
The Silent Prayer and Meditation

THE WORD OF COMMITMENT . . .
Love Is Acceptable to God
"Father, into thy hands I commit my spirit."

The Scripture Reading *Luke 23:44-49*
The Meditation on the Seventh Word
The Prayer

Father in Heaven, we would express our gratitude to you for revealing the greatness of your salvation for man through the Christ and his death on Calvary. May the cross become for us a symbol of your love and concern for man. Sustain us as we would attempt to carry our own cross through life, and challenge us that we might be faithful to you to the end, through Jesus Christ our Lord. Amen.

The Hymn
The Silent Prayer and Meditation
The Benediction
The Postlude

‡‡‡‡‡

A SERVICE OF JOY AND PRAISE FOR EASTER

Prelude

Call to Worship

Minister: Christ is risen!
People: He is risen indeed!
Minister: He lives today.
People: He lives within us.
Minister: Alleluia!
People: Alleluia! Alleluia!

Hymn of Praise

Invocation

Almighty God, we offer our praise to you in the spirit of joy and thankfulness. We are grateful for your coming to earth in the form of Jesus Christ, and revealing yourself through him. We are especially thankful for the gift of salvation, given through his death upon the cross, and the promise of eternal life, revealed through his resurrection. As the dawning of Easter morning brought new hope to the followers of Christ, we pray that you will bring joy and hope to our hearts this day, in the name of the risen Christ. Amen.

Prayer of Confession

Eternal God, our Father, we are mindful of the disciples and their lack of loyalty during the trial and crucifixion of our Lord, and we confess that we have also failed you. We have placed you on trial before our friends and associates, and sometimes we have deserted you. In times of decision, when to witness would have required us to take a firm stand for you through our betrayal. Grant us forgiveness of all of our sins, as you forgave the disciples, and bring new hope to our hearts, as you did to them on that first Easter, in the name of Jesus Christ our Lord. Amen.

Words of Assurance

The God of the Resurrection grants you full pardon for all your sins and commissions you to go forth and be a blessing to all who cross your way this day.

May his Spirit abide in your life, giving new freedom and power to live by his direction and to his satisfaction. Amen.

Lord's Prayer

Affirmation of Faith

We believe in one God, maker and ruler of all things, Father of all men, the source of all goodness and beauty, all truth and love.

We believe in Jesus Christ, God manifest in the flesh, our teacher, example, and redeemer, the Savior of the world.

We believe in the Holy Spirit, God present with us for guidance, for comfort, and for strength.

We believe in the forgiveness of sins, in the life of love and prayer, and in grace equal to every need.

We believe in the Word of God contained in the Old and New Testaments as the sufficient rule of faith and practice.

We believe in the Church as the fellowship for worship and for service of all who are united to the living Lord.

We believe in the Kingdom of God as the divine rule in human society, and in the brotherhood of man under the fatherhood of God.

We believe in the triumph of righteousness, and in the life everlasting. Amen.

Easter Anthem

Easter Story in Scripture

Minister: On the first day of the week, at early dawn, they went to the tomb taking the spices which they had prepared. And they found the stone rolled away from the tomb.

People: Alleluia!

Minister: So they departed quickly from the tomb with fear and great joy, and ran to tell his disciples. And behold, Jesus met them and said, "Hail!"

People: Alleluia!

Minister: But Mary stood weeping outside the tomb. She said, "They have taken away my Lord, and I do not know where they have laid him." Saying this, she saw Jesus standing, but did not know that it was Jesus. Jesus said to her, "Mary." She turned and said to him, "Master."

People: *Alleluia!*

Minister: Two of them were going to Emmaus; and Jesus drew near and went with them. But their eyes were kept from recognizing him. When he was at the table with them, their eyes were opened and they recognized him.

People: *Alleluia!*

Minister: On the evening of that day, the doors being shut where the disciples were, Jesus came and stood among them and said to them, "Peace be with you."

People: *Alleluia!*

Easter Prayer

Eternal God of resurrection power, we approach this morning filled with wonder and awe. Why have you chosen to redeem us, we ask? We, who have only looked for ways to betray are now called into the presence of a redeeming Lord and Savior. Our hope this day is complete with the knowledge that even our last enemy has fallen to your conquering power. Grant us new faith to absorb this amazing love. We, the children of God, affirm our belief that you have granted new life not as a favor or reward, but as the means by which your community on earth and heaven shall be a reality. May your blessing this day be a reminder to us all that we are living not only in time but also in eternity. These are the prayers of your people who pray in the name of Christ Jesus. Amen.

Litany of Celebration

Minister: Christ has risen from the dead.

People: *Let's celebrate his resurrection.*

Minister: The risen Christ conquered death to bring new life to man.

People: Let's celebrate the newness of life.

Minister: The spirit of the risen Christ is in our midst.

People: Let's celebrate his abiding presence.

Minister: The risen Christ challenges us to witness to the world.

People: Let's celebrate his life through our daily witness.

Minister: The Spirit of the risen Christ brings joy to our hearts.

People: Let's celebrate with joy and praise.

Hymn of Celebration

Easter Offering

Doxology

Easter Meditation

Words of Triumph

Minister: Go forth and tell everyone that Christ is risen!

People: We will tell them that he triumphed over death and the grave.

Minister: Tell them that his spirit is alive in the world today.

People: We will praise him with our words and our deeds. Alleluia!

Hymn of Triumph

Benediction

Postlude

Service of the Upper Room
Thomas W. Lentz

The lessons for both Maundy Thursday and Good Friday contain several references to the Passover. Many are unaware of the connection between the Last Supper and the Passover Celebration. This meditation gives historical perspective to the sacrament by relating it to the earlier Jewish festival and thus provides a deeper understanding and appreciation for Holy Communion.

In order to more vividly illustrate the sermon, there are suggested places for the use of chalice, loaf of bread, green vegetable, basin, and towels.

Sections of the sermon are taken from the Jewish Passover festival, but it is by no means complete. The author has simply taken those parts that have the closest associations to the Last Supper or relate most specifically to Christian teaching and custom.

Old Testament Lesson	Exodus 12:1-4
Epistle Lesson	1 Corinthians 11:20-32
Gospel Lesson	John 13:1-15

The sacredness of eating together in fellowship has a history much older than Holy Communion. Our Lord Jesus was not instituting a brand new custom when he brought his disciples together for that Last Supper. Jesus was a good Jew and recognized that most important event in Jewish worship, the Passover festival. Only when we realize the rich and significant history behind the Last Supper, do we come to appreciate even more the special meaning of Holy Communion which we receive around the altar.

Tonight we shall recall those events which occurred more than three thousand years ago, the Egyptian bondage of the children of Israel and their deliverance by God.

Human history is marked with those black pages which record the enslavement of peoples by tyrants. But the Israelites were the first to rebel against serfdom and to establish a religious festival dedicated to freedom. On the day of the Passover feast every Jewish home becomes a sanctuary and every table an altar where gratitude is expressed to God, the author of liberty.

In the Passover celebration, each item on the table has a religious significance. The festival begins with the invocation of God's name and the filling of the first of four cups of wine. Wine in the East is as common a beverage as tea or coffee are for us. [*At this point, you may fill a chalice with wine, or simply hold up the chalice.*]

The traditional words of praise are then proclaimed: *Praised be thou, O Lord our God, King of the Universe, Creator of the fruit of the vine. Praised be thou, O Lord our God, King of universe, who didst choose us from among all people for thy service, and exalted us by teaching us holiness through thy commandments.*

One cannot come before God's Holiness without remembering his command of obedience. We are reminded of St. Paul's exhortation: "Let a man examine himself, and so eat the bread and drink of the cup. For any one who eats and drinks without discerning the body eats and drinks judgment upon himself." (1 Corinthians 11:28-29)

Having drunk the first cup of wine, the custom of the Passover celebration is then to pass a pitcher of water with basin and towels so that all may wash their hands. [*You may at this time hold up basin and towels.*] It was to this event that Jesus gave new meaning when he himself "began to wash the disciples' feet, and to wipe them with the towel with which he was girded." (John 13:5) By this act our Lord showed that no task is too humble for a Christian. "You call me Lord and Teacher; and you are right, for so I am. If I then, your Lord and Teacher, have washed your feet, you also ought to wash one another's feet. For I have given you an example, that you also should do as I have done to you." (John 13:13-15)

The Passover celebration proceeds with the eating of a green vegetable, the symbol of springtime. [*You may have present for display a green vegetable such as the head of lettuce to draw attention to this part of the festival.*] While we do not include this in our sacrament of Communion, we recognize green as the symbol of renewal when we display the green paraments during Trinity Season.

For thousands of years bread has been the staple diet of man. In the East it was especially important. It is, therefore, a central item in the feast of the Passover. [*You may display here a loaf of bread.*] The daily meal always included one loaf of bread; but on the Sabbath two loaves are set out as a reminder of the double portion of manna which fell on Friday for the children of Israel as they traveled in the wilderness. (Exodus 16:22) In honor of the Passover, a third loaf was added. The leader of the celebration uncovers the bread, lifts up the ceremonial plate and says: *Behold the matzah, bread of poverty, which our ancestors ate in the land of Egypt. Let all who are hungry come and eat: all who are needy, come and celebrate the Passover with us.*

Jesus, while reminding us that "man shall not live by bread alone" (Matthew 4:4) also taught us to recognize the source of all our nourishment when he told us to pray to God for our daily bread. (Matthew 6:11)

Perhaps all of our eating and drinking should take on a sacramental character, but we recognize especially in Holy Communion "that the Lord Jesus on the night when he was betrayed took bread, and when he had given thanks, he broke it and said, "This is my body which is for you. Do this in remembrance of me!" (1 Corinthians 11:23b-24)

In the Passover celebration, the youngest child or a

guest asks the question, "Why is this night different from all other nights?" And the leader answers:

1. On all other nights we may eat either leavened or unleavened bread, but on this night only unleavened bread, because when our ancestors were told by Pharoah that they could leave Egypt, they had no time to bake bread with leaven, so they baked it without leaven.
2. On all other nights we eat all kinds of herbs, but on this night we eat especially bitter herbs in order to remind us of the bitterness our ancestors experienced when they were oppressed by the Egyptian taskmaster.
3. On all other nights, we need not even once dip our herbs in any condiment but on this night we dip herbs twice; one herb in salt water, and the bitter herbs in haroset. This is to remind us that the Egyptians embittered the lives of our forefathers in Egypt as the Bible explains: "They made their lives bitter with hard labor, with mortar and brick and with every kind of work in the field. All the labor which the Egyptians forced upon them was harsh." (Exodus 1:14)
4. On all other nights we eat either sitting or reclining, but on this night we recline. This is a sign of our freedom. For in antiquity the slaves ate hurriedly, standing or squatting on the ground, while royalty, nobility, and the wealthy in Egypt, Persia, Rome, and other empires dined on couches. To indicate the freedom that has been won, we recline while eating.

Praised be God: praised be he: praised be he who gave the Torah to his people Israel: praised be he.

We Christians here gathered tonight are the heirs of a long and rich history. We are the chosen people of God; chosen to receive his promise and with it the command of obedience. This is the God who has said, I have given you as a covenant to the people, a light to the nations, to open the eyes of the blind. . . . We have an important part to play in the plans of our God who is directing the course of human events toward their fulfillment when he shall come again to judge each man.

As we look back through the pages of our Christian ancestry we perceive a God who is actively involved in the lives of his people.

A young girl asked the question recently, "How can I ever believe that God has always existed, that he has never had a beginning, because he has always been?"

The answer to such a probing question is not easy to communicate to a young mind. But there is an answer that would go something like this: Time is a human category. We think in terms of time, because we are humans who are limited by it. Our minds cannot conceive of a timeless Being because even our minds and intellects are restricted and limited to concepts such as time. But God is above time; he created time. He is not human, he is above and beyond such human concepts. Therefore, we cannot describe God in human concepts.

This desire to describe God to ourselves and others sometimes places us in a real dilemma. For when we talk about him our language gets muddled and broken and we are bound to sound even self-contradictory.

How many times do we proclaim that the Church is the Body of Christ? Therefore it is obedient unto Christ, the light of the nations, opening the eyes of the blind. But then some young penetrating eyes come along and ask, "Where?" Where is that church? Where is that body showing men the light, the way of life, dying to the world to show the true life of Christ, the unity of his body?

So we get into trouble if we become terribly, terribly honest. Our words become distorted. We raise questions and make compromises. The problem is that the contradictions are part of our human frailty, not part of God's nature.

Yes, we have a terrible time trying to explain and understand the divinity and majesty of God, and that makes it difficult for us to speak *about* God. That must be why he came to speak to us; that must be why he lowered himself to take on flesh of our flesh, so that he could speak to us and we *to* him, not simply *about* him.

God recognizes that we are not all mind and intellect. We are beings who also move and respond to our senses, to our emotions. And so God does not simply confront us with his word, but he also comes down to touch us, using his own created elements of bread and wine.

And so now it is time for us to come and receive his broken body, his spilled blood. We come on bended knee to divest ourselves of our weaknesses, our errors, our follies. We throw ourselves entirely at his mercy and he, the great Judge of all mankind, answers: "Take and eat, this is my body, given for thee. Take, drink, this is my blood, shed for thee."

Holy Week Tenebrae
William Luther White

This service is an adaptation of the ancient Tenebrae (Shadow) Service. The ceremony of gradually extinguishing candles to dramatize the fading Light of the World has been used in the Church since the Eighth Century. In English medieval churches, twenty-four candles were used in the service. The service requires three days of Holy Week in the Roman Church. Though the basic idea for this service is twelve centuries old, the following materials have been assembled particularly for this presentation. The descriptions of the disciples are based upon *These Twelve*, a book by Charles R. Brown.

The altar is draped in black and holds one large candle, already lighted, accompanied by twelve smaller, unlighted candles.

I. THE PROLOGUE

Organ Prelude

Call to Worship — *Isaiah 9:2*

Hymn — "Alas! and Did My Savior Bleed" #415

II. THE COMING OF CHRIST INTO THE WORLD

Responsive Reading — Sentences from John 1 and 1 John 1

Minister: Christ is the light of the world! As we observe the lighted Christ candle, let us remember these words from the Fourth Gospel: "The true light that enlightens every man was coming into the world. He was in the world, and the world was made through him, yet the world knew him not.

People: *"There was a man sent from God, whose name was John. He came for testimony, to bear witness to the Light, that all might believe through him. He was not the light, but came to bear witness to the light."*

Minister: Elsewhere, we read: "This is the message

we have heard from him and proclaim to you, that God is light, and in him is no darkness at all.

People: *"If we say we have fellowship with him while we walk in darkness, we lie and do not live according to the truth; but if we walk in the light, as he is in the light, we have fellowship with one another . . ."*

III. THE CALLING OF THE APOSTLES

"YOU Are the Light" Sentences from Matthew 5

The gospels tell us that Jesus called to himself twelve apostles. These men, too, are represented by lighted candles. Jesus spoke to them, and to us also, when he said:

"*You* are the light of the world. A city set on a hill cannot be hid. Nor do men light a lamp and put it under a bushel, but on a stand, and it gives light to all in the house. Let your light so shine before men, that they may see your good works and give glory to your Father who is in heaven."

Lighting of the Apostles' Candles

Jesus called *Simon Peter* to be a disciple . . .* [*Light appropriate candle*] He also called his brother, *Andrew* . . .*

"As Jesus walked by the Sea of Galilee, he saw two brothers, Simon who is called Peter and Andrew his brother, casting a net into the sea: for they were fishermen. And he said to them, "Follow me, and I will make you fishers of men." Immediately they left their nets and followed him . . ."

Jesus called *James* to be a disciple . . .* He called also his brother *John* . . .*

"And going on from these he saw two other brothers, James, the son of Zebedee and John his brother, in the boat with Zebedee, their father, mending their nets, and he called them. Immediately they left the boat and their father, and followed him."

Jesus called *Matthew* to be a disciple . . .*

"Jesus went out and saw a tax collector, named Levi, sitting at the tax office; and he said to him, 'Follow me.' And he left everything and rose and followed him."

[*Organ background music may begin at this point: "Rise Up, O Men of God"*]

Jesus called *Thomas* to be his disciple . . .* He also called *Simon*, the Zealot . . .*

Jesus called *Philip* . . .*

He called also *Judas Iscariot* . . .*

Jesus called *James*, the son of Alphaeus, *Bartholomew*, and *Thaddeus* . . .*

Charge to the Apostles Sentences from Matthew 10

Jesus sent his Apostles forth, charging them: "Preach as you go, saying, 'The kingdom of heaven is at hand.' Heal the sick, raise the dead, cleanse lepers, cast out demons. You received without pay, give without pay, give without pay. . . . Behold, I send you out as sheep in the midst of wolves; so be wise as serpents and innocent as doves. Beware of men; for they will deliver you up to councils, and flog you in their synagogues, and you will be dragged before governors and kings for my sake, to bear testimony before them and the Gentiles. When they deliver you up, do not be anxious how you are to speak or what you are to say; for what you are to say will be given to you in that hour; for it is not you who speak, but the Spirit of your Father speaking through you. . . . Everyone who acknowledges me before me, I also will acknowledge before my father."

[*House lights half on*]

Communion

IV. THE GARDEN OF GETHSEMANE

Introduction to the Scene

The mood and the scene shift now. After several months of intimate fellowship and training, Jesus has returned with his disciple band to Jerusalem and to the garden outside the city walls known as Gethsemane. The group has just shared together in the Last

Supper in the Upper Room, and Jesus has announced his impending betrayal and death. [*Exit Judas*]

Imagine now a scene in the Garden of Gethsemane as Jesus leads in prayer and spends his final moments on earth among his disciples. Imagine, too, some of the troubled thoughts that must have gone through his disciples' minds on this fateful night.

Hymn "'Tis Midnight"

Jesus' Prayer for His Followers From John 17

"Father, the hour has come; glorify thy Son. . . . Holy Father, keep them in thy name which thou hast given me, that they may be one, even as we are one. While I was with them, I kept them. . . . I have guarded them. But now I am coming to thee. I do not pray that thou shouldst take them out of the world, but that thou shouldst keep them from evil. Sanctify them in the truth. . . . As thou didst send me into the world, I have sent them into the world. I will make (thy name) known, that the love with which thou has loved me may be in them, and I in them."

Reflections of Jesus' Disciples Off-stage voices

[*House lights one quarter on*]

Bartholomew

How still the evening. Only a faint breeze stirs the olive branches tonight. Yet there is a strange foreboding in the air. It's too still — like the quiet before a mighty storm. . . . How long can this last? Every day to the city, every night to this garden. The tension mounts. Sooner or later we'll surely be found. Our hideout will be discovered. And what then? They touch the Master in daytime when the crowd is all about. But out here on this barren hillside — who would ever know? The soldiers, the spies, of Caesar are everywhere. What if they *do* come here? Could a dozen men stand off the Roman Army? Oh, to be back on the peaceful slopes of Galilee! I trust our Master, but I do not always understand him! Why did we come back to Jerusalem now? Why now?

Andrew

"Fishers of men" it has been these recent months! How the crowds have hung on his words. He has spoken with authority, unlike the others. They have listened by the thousands — children and old folks, nobles and lepers. They have all come, and their lives have been enriched by a touch or a word from him. How my own life has been changed! I knew nothing but fish, and mending nets, before he came our way. Now — how can I express it — I feel chosen to serve a King, to labor in the very Kingdom of Heaven! How I remember that day when he came down to our boat, as intent as a commander gathering his troops. "Andrew," he said, "follow me." I could not refuse, I could not resist. There was a compulsion in his voice, a fire in his eyes that I could not deny. I had to follow him, to find out more about him, and finally to serve him! Beginning with my own brother Peter, it has been my privilege to introduce many to Christ. Never for a moment have I regretted that decision — to throw down my nets and to become a fisher of men!

James

Was it only a week ago that we paraded through the city gate? A week ago? Yes . . . hardly that long. You'd have thought the whole city was turning out. Palm branches, songs, gaiety, the laughter of children. . . . How fortune changed! The parade was fit for a king. At least it would have been if we'd had a magnificent horse instead of that stupid donkey. Still, it was a fine parade. Now, we sneak around at dusk like hunted animals. The soldiers and the Pharisees try to trap us into saying something for which they can arrest us – fomenting rebellion against Caesar or something. . . . Jesus was outwitted them so far. He's on to their tricks. Ah, it's a joy to see him work. "Master, shall we pay taxes to Caesar or not?" "Give back to Caesar what is rightfully his — but return to God what belongs to him." A splendid answer! But the officials didn't think so. How they wish he'd walk into one of their traps! How they wish they knew where he spent his evenings! A knock on the door at midnight — then all would fall silent. No more embarrassing scenes of healing in the marketplace, no more criticisms of the way things have always been done, no more mighty pronouncements in the name of God. Just quiet. They'd like to get him. They'd like to . . .

Thomas

It seemed like the right thing to say at the time. Now I'm not so sure. Was I wise or was I foolhardy? I suppose I'm as responsible as anyone for our being here now. I wonder if the others remember. I was so bold at first when it became clear Jesus intended to come back to Jerusalem. We all recognized the danger. But it was *I* who spoke up and said, "Then let us all go back to Jerusalem to die with him!" Brave words! It's easier to be brave down in Galilee. But now? I know, I need not air my doubts. The others would say to me, as they've said before, "Thomas, you're so skeptical!" It is true that Jesus seems to be chosen by God for some great cause. We have daily seen his mighty works. He teaches with a strange authority. But what good can possibly come from this place? Jerusalem! Gethsemane! Can it be that Jesus has finally made a mistake — a mistake that will end it all forever? God is with us, they say. But where's the proof? It doesn't make sense. Did he come here — to the very valley of the shadow of death — to speak of God's love and power? Why indeed!?

Matthew

It's amazing when you think of it? Who but Jesus would have chosen such a motley band as us twelve and expected us to get along? Not only to get along together, but to become a radiant fellowship of harmony and love. . . . Ah, the difference he has made in our lives in these short months! There I was —

Matthew the tax collector. Most of my own countrymen hated me for my job with the occupation government. "Matthew — that old Roman!" they used to say with contempt. Well, I knew where the money was, and decided to get my share of it. They called me traitor, but the pay was excellent. That is, I thought it was until I met Jesus and began to hear about treasurers of the heart and treasures in heaven. Little by little, I began to discover that money had actually been my god! I understand when Jesus said, "No man can serve two masters; you cannot serve God and money." It is truly remarkable that he could expect me — a money-conscious Roman sympathizer — to live peaceable day by day with a man like Simon, that fierce Zealot patriot. He called Peter, the impetuous one, and James the quiet one. Not to mention those brothers who were known all about us as the "sons of thunder." Amazing! And yet under his teaching and influence, we have found our disagreements melting away. We have practiced forgiveness. And we have grown together in a loyalty deeper than life itself. Thanks be to God for this man Jesus!

John

How heavy our hearts were at supper tonight. This wasn't the way Peter and I had expected it when we engaged the room. We had planned for the traditional Passover feast, yes — but we didn't know things would turn out like this. How sad it made us to hear him speak of his approaching death as though it were inevitable. "This is the last time we shall break bread together." "This cup represents my blood . . ." "This is my body, broken for you . . ." Tears welled up in my eyes at the very thought of parting with our Master. But he tells us that these things must come to pass that God may be glorified. *How* can God be glorified in our losing the best Friend we've ever known? *How* can God be glorified in Israel's losing her greatest Teacher? Thousands have been touched already by his words and healing power. Must it end so early? Will it all come to nothing? He seems drawn to death like a lamb marked for slaughter. Can God *possibly* use this for any good purpose?

Philip

All of us were stunned by his words at table tonight. "One of *you,*" he said, "will betray me." One of *us!* Why, that's incredible! Why would one of us — his chosen disciples, his key pupils — harm our Master? We've been through so much together, eaten together, walked together, talked together, prayed together. *Could* one of us do such a thing. Betrayal? I watched the faces of the others. They were as astonished as I. But after the initial shock, we each began to reconsider. Jesus is not accustomed to being mistaken or to speaking lightly. Surely he knew what he was talking about. Did he know something within our hearts that we ourselves have not yet discovered? One after another, we began to ask him. Painful though it was, we had to know. "Is it *I*, Lord? Is it *I?*" We would as nearly suspect ourselves as any other man of our circle. Jesus did not answer directly. "It is one," he said, "who dipped his hand in the dish with me." Who did that? Did I? . . . Oh, God, let *me* not have anything to do with betrayal. . . . Let me remain loyal!

James, Son of Alphaeus

Never have I seen our Lord appear more troubled. It's not that warm, but perspiration was dripping from his brow before he left us now. He bit deep into his lip, gazed steadily at us, and said, "Watch with me — and pray! My soul is very sorrowful tonight — sorrowful unto death." As we sat down, he went up that slope and hurled himself face downward in prayer. Such agony — as though his heart would break. We ache to see him thus, but we know that he would not have it otherwise. He knew the risk. But he *would* not be dissuaded from marching straight into Jerusalem itself — the very bastion of the forces of evil. I recall his exact words when we reversed our journey. He called the twelve of us aside and made the announcement: "Behold," he said, "we are going up to Jerusalem. The Son of man will be delivered to the chief priests and scribes, and they will condemn him to death, and deliver him to the Gentiles to be mocked and scourged and crucified. And he will be raised on the third day." Whatever he meant by all that, that *is* what he said. In sorrow or joy, Jesus trusts the guidance of our loving heavenly Father. I do not always understand everything Jesus says and does. But I've seen enough to pledge him my devotion and my life.

Peter

It hurts to have your loyalty questioned. I wish Jesus hadn't been so blunt with me this evening. He's worried, of course, and his mind is burdened with many things. But he doesn't understand *me*. I tried to assure him of my support, whatever happens. I said, "Lord, though the others will fall away because of you, I will *never* fall away." Why couldn't he just take my word for it? No, instead, he turned to me with sorrow-filled eyes and said, "Peter — before sunrise you will deny that you ever knew me." How those words cut! And then I came near to losing my temper. Firmly, I insisted again, "Lord, even if I must *die* with you, I will not deny you!" Do I still seem to him like shifting sand? I'm determined to become a Rock, for which I am named. I know, I've sometimes been impetuous and hotheaded in the past. But I'm changing. I am! Others have noted it, too. . . . Come here tonight, Centurion, and you'll have *me* to answer to. You'll find a Big Fisherman who's become a Man of Stone. My sword is sharp, and there shall be no retreat for *this* disciple. Though I pour out my blood on this very spot, I will not deny my Lord! Others may fail, but not *I!* Not *I!*

Thaddeus

Oh, how weary I am. So terribly sleepy. My bones creak with exhaustion. And yet I should spend more time in prayer. Our Master is depending on us. It's such a crucial time for him. He needs our prayers. But how can I keep going much longer? The pace this week has been rugged for the strongest of us. No one complains, of course, but I've noticed how tired some of them are. I was embarrassed at supper tonight; in the warmth of that upper room, I though my eyelids would collapse, even during the meal. I'll try once more. I'll try to pray longer. But God forgive me if my brain goes numb and I fall asleep . . .

Simon, the Zealot

It seems that Judas and I have had more trouble understanding Jesus than the others. It's due to our Zealot background, I suppose. For years, we've been taught that the overthrow of Rome would come by violence. There was a time when we both carried daggers in our sleeves — just in case we needed them fast. But Jesus' methods are so different. He's utterly contrary to our expectations. He's said it a hundred ways, I'm sure — though I'm just beginning to realize it — that his Kingdom is a Kingdom of the heart — not a Kingdom of marching armies and drawn swords. It seems like such a slow, tedious way to combat evil! Judas and I especially need to be very patient with this new approach. I'm not sure Judas understands it fully yet. Only last week, as we returned to Jerusalem, he said to me, "Perhaps *now*. Perhaps now Jesus will face the armies of Rome and call legions of angels into battle!" "No," said I, "I don't think so. That's just not his way." I wonder where Judas is now? . . . We must learn to be very patient. We must all learn patience.

The Falling Away of the Apostles" From John 18

[*House lights off*]

Judas, procuring a band of soldiers and some

officers from the chief priests and the Pharisees, went there with lanterns and torches and weapons. Then Jesus, knowing all that was to befall him, came forward and said to them, "Whom do you seek?" They answered him, "Jesus of Nazareth." "I am he." Judas, who betrayed him, was standing with them. When he said to them, "I am he," they drew back and fell to the ground. Again he asked them, "Whom do you seek?" And they said, "Jesus of Nazareth." Jesus answered, "I told you that I am he; so if you seek me, let these men go."

Simon Peter followed Jesus. . . . Now Peter was standing and warming himself. They said to him, "Are you not also one of his disciples?" He denied it and said, "I am not." One of the servants of the high priest, a kinsman of the man whose ear Peter had cut off, asked, "Did I not see you in the garden with him?" Peter again denied it; and at once the cock crowed.

[*Exit – Peter candle*]

And Jesus was taken out to the place of the skull, called Golgotha, to be crucified.

V. THE CRUCIFIXION

Jesus' Final Words From John 19

At the words, "It is finished," the altar light and all artificial lights should be extinguished; only the flame of the Christ candle remains. As the Christ candle is then extinguished, a shadow of a huge cross may appear above the altar, by having arranged a small cross in the beams of a spotlight (or slide projector) in the balcony.

The ministers may kneel at the altar under the shadow of the cross for a few moments before slowly and quietly moving out, followed by the choir a moment later. *There is no other conclusion to the service, with a dead Christ, there is nothing more to say until Easter morning.*

Choir Possibilities, at appropriate points in the service

1. "The Passion According to St. John" by de Victoria-Lovelace
2. "Messiah" (portions of it) by Handel
3. "Is It Nothing to You?" by Robert Powell
4. "Beneath the Cross of Jesus"

Standing on Golgotha
Thomas W. Lentz

Lessons

Isaiah 53:4-12
Revelation 15:1-14
John 18:1-19:42

[*The notations included in parenthesis are simply included to convey the author's impression of how the narrative sections of the sermon might be expressed.*]

Come with me for the next few moments and view the events that are taking place in Jerusalem. If we stand here together in Golgotha we can observe all the action without getting caught in the press of the crowd.

How surprising it is to suddenly realize that within our view here on Golgotha are the Mount of Olives, the Garden of Gethsemane, the Kidron Valley, and the Golden Gates through which Jesus made his triumphal entry only a few days ago. All the places where the major events occurred are visible to us from here.

[*Squint eyes as though looking at something in the rear of the church.*] But look, down there on the city streets! The crowd is rapidly growing. Why do so many seem to enjoy seeing a man suffer? They're taunting him. It's despicable.

[*Pause as if in reflection.*] These last few days have been so frustrating. The message of Jesus has given my entire life new meaning. I intended to join his disciples and follow him . . . and now this. It's been very strange, though. In fact, Jesus has been rather strange about it. We all kept trying to work out a strategy to avoid this inevitable confrontation. But Jesus would have none of our plans. It was as though he intended it to happen this way. At least he didn't take any steps to avoid what we all saw was coming.

And now look at him. How could anyone endure what he is going through?

They're getting closer. Why, that's a regular mob around him with some of the most respectable people in the community mingling right in with those scoundrels who turn out for anything that has violence connected with it. And listen to them! They're in a frenzy! These are decent God-fearing people, even some of the Temple officials — and they're all screaming at the top of their lungs, "Crucify him, crucify him, crucify him." [*Spoken softly, fading out with last two words, as though in deep contemplation.*]

Can you imagine?

Can you imagine sending your only son, who has obeyed you and has served you willingly, into a crowd of fiends, anxiously awaiting to kill him? You have to admit that you couldn't do it; nor could I. It makes you wonder what God is that he could do it. What strength of will he has to accomplish his purpose.

How often I have read it in scripture, yet it never really meant a whole lot until now when I have to behold it before my very eyes.

The words went:

Surely he has borne our griefs
  and carried our sorrows;
yet we esteemed him stricken,
  smitten by God, and afflicted.

(Isaiah 53:4)

Imagine!

Imagine yourself listening to your son as he kneels at your feet, asking you if you can provide any other way besides the slow agony of a death with spikes ripping the flesh of hands and feet, and turning your head away in steady determination. Do you think that you could stand such anguish? It makes you wonder about God, who could and did stand such anguish. Think of the unrelenting power of his resolutions!

Isaiah put it correctly:

But he was wounded for our transgressions,
  he was bruised for our iniquities;

upon him was the chastisement that made us
whole,
and with his stripes we are healed.
(Isaiah 53:5)

Imagine yourself sending your only son into a group of people, hoping that the message you have given him will be listened to since it is for their benefit and their welfare; and imagine watching as they whip him, laugh at him, and nail him on the cross he's carrying. Wouldn't you, if you had the power, shout out before they tortured your son, "Stop the scene, it mustn't go any further." And yet here it is all happening before our very eyes. Think about the determination God has to make his ways known.

He was oppressed, and he was afflicted,
yet he opened not his mouth;
like a lamb that is led to the slaughter,
and like a sheep that before its shearers is
dumb,
so he opened not his mouth.
(Isaiah 53:7)

But finally, imagine yourself letting all this happen to your only son, innocent of any crime, for the very souls of those down there who are torturing him, so that they will not have to bear the consequences of their evil deeds. Think about what depth of compassion, what strength of love God must have.

All we like sheep have gone astray;
we have turned every one to his own way;
And the Lord has laid on him the iniquity of us all.
(Isaiah 53:6)

How many years, yes, how many centuries, have we been asking if the whole meaning and purpose of human life is to be capped by nothing better than the violence of death, or a vague state of nothingness in Sheol? How long have we been asking, "Is man to struggle through infancy and adolescence, scramble all through his middle years only to have all his efforts rewarded by his own extinction?"

I wonder if people realize that the answer is being given them right here before their very eyes? That God himself is here today sharing with us this human experience of death, even in its most tragic form. If he does that it means we are not separated from him by death. We can reach out and grasp his nail-pierced hands, knowing that death is not separation but merely the prelude to an eternal fellowship with him.

I wonder if people in times to come will ever look back and say, "The sacrifice was too great." What a wonder it is that God does not look upon this mob today and draw that conclusion. How greatly he must value us to sacrifice his own son!

I recall now several months ago a crowd had gathered to hear Jesus talk. He was telling them how much God cared for them, each one of them. He said that God knew each one of them infinitely better than they knew themselves. "I know my own and my own known me," he said. "And I lay down my life for my sheep."

They've reached the summit now, a little distance from where we're standing. My heart goes out to him. What can I do to help? His poor mother and a few disciples are watching from a distance.

O my God, my God, they're spiking his hands to the wood. His groans of pain are more than I can bear.

O Lord Jesus, can it be? Have I too caused you this suffering and this pain?

All we like sheep have gone astray;
we have turned every one to his own way;
and the Lord has laid on him the iniquity of us all.
And I lay down my life for my sheep.

Yes, we are just as guilty as those driving the nails. When our bitter tongues have lashed out against one another, when our thankless hearts have taken life for granted, when our evil minds have gone astray and bred hatred, when we have demanded from others instead of giving to others, we, too, have had our hands on the mallet which drives spikes and wedges into God's love.

We, too, have consented to and participated in the same demonic spirit which has ravished this crowd.

I can hear his words, "Inasmuch as you either loved or hated a small child, a husband or wife, a mother or father, a friend or even an enemy, you either loved or hated me."

All we like sheep have gone astray.

Is that to be the final judgment? Will this be God's final act of condemnation that will hand over our heads for centuries, searing our consciences?

But wait! Did you hear what he said?

Father, forgive them, for they know not what
they do.

Will the world ever hear the words of this dying man? Will it listen?

Here we stand before our Lord's broken body, his spilled blood; a judgment on us all. And yet he has still accepted us all in his fold.

Come, let us descend from the hill, for the spirit of the Lord is upon us. He sends us forth to bind up the broken-hearted, to proclaim liberty to the captives, to bring release to those who are bound in the captivity of their ways.

Good Friday Service
E. E. Olson

Introduction

Choir "When Jesus Wept"
"God So Loved the World" (Stainer)

Narrator

This is where it all starts, with the love of God.

Reader A

Thus says the Lord:
"I will betroth you to me in faithfulness; and you
shall know the Lord . . .
And I will have pity on 'Not Pitied,'
and I will say to 'Not my people,'
'You are my people . . .' "
Thus says the Lord:
"Incline your ear, and come to me;
hear that your soul may live;
and I will make with you an everlasting covenant,
my steadfast, sure love for David."
"And I, John, heard a great voice from the throne saying,
"Behold, the dwelling of God is with men, he will
dwell with them,
and they shall be his people, and God himself will
be with them.' "

Narrator

Love could not be contained.
Love cannot be hemmed in.
Love *must* spill out.
In no place we know of did God say it in so many words, in the Holy Scripture. But the Christian thinkers have asked, and continue to ask, the reason God made man in the first place. The answer that seems satisfying to some people is that God made man because God's own love had

to have an object. God felt an inner compulsion to show his love. God had to give his love. Mankind is the result.

Reader B [*Two youth*]

The Word of God says:

See what manner of love the Father has given us, that we should be called the children of God; and so we are . . .

He who does right is righteous, as he is righteous.

He who commits sin is of the devil; for the devil has sinned from the beginning. The reason the Son of God appeared was to destroy the works of the devil.

By this it may be seen who are the children of God, and who are the children of the devil; whoever does not do right is not of God, nor he who does not love his brother.

But if anyone has the world's goods and sees his brother in need, yet closes his heart against him, how does God's love abide in him? Little children, let us not love just in word or speech, but in deed and in truth.

Beloved, let us love one another; for love is of God, and he who loves is born of God and knows God. He who does not love does not know God; for God is love.

In this the love of God was manifest among us, that God sent his only son into the world, so that we might live through him. In this is love, not that we loved God, but that he loved us and sent his Son to be the expiation for our sins.

In this is love perfected with us, that we may have confidence for the day of judgment. . . . There is no fear in love, perfect love casts out fear.

We love because he first loved us.

Choir "Behold the Lamb of God"

Narrator

He takes away the sins of the world.

But how?

Reader A

The Scripture says:
that "Christ cleansed the Church by the washing of water with the Word."
It says that those who "came out of the great tribulation have washed their robes and made them white in the blood of the Lamb."

Narrator

The night before he was betrayed he washed the feet of the disciples, and in the course of the evening he said that "he who has bathed does not need to wash except for his feet, but he is clean all over; and you are clean, but not all of you."

Reader C

Thus says the Lord:
" . . . declare to my people their transgression.
Yet they seek me daily,
and delight to know my ways,
as if they were a nation that did righteousness
and did not forsake the ordinance of their God;
they ask of me righteous judgments,
they delight to draw near to God.
They say,
'Why have we fasted, and thou seest it not?
Why have we humbled ourselves, and thou takest no knowledge of it?'
Here is why I do not hear:
Behold, in the day of your fast you seek your own pleasure,
and oppress all your workers.
Behold, you fast only to quarrel and to fight
and to hit with wicked fist.
Fasting like yours this day will not make your voice heard on high.
Is such the fast that I choose?
a day for a man to humble himself?
Is it to bow down his head like a rush,
and to spread sackcloth and ashes under him?

Will you call this a fast,
    and a day acceptable to the Lord?
Is not this rather the fast that I choose:
    to loose the bonds of wickedness,
    to undo the thongs of the yoke,
    to let the oppressed go free
        and to break every yoke?
Is it not to share your bread with the hungry,
    and bring the homeless poor into your house;
    when you see the naked, to cover him,
    and not hide yourself from your own flesh?
If you do this:
Then shall your light break forth like the dawn,
    and your healing shall spring up speedily;
    your righteousness shall go before you,
        the glory of the Lord shall be your rear guard.
Then shall you call, and the Lord will answer;
    You shall cry, and he will say, 'Here . . . I . . . am!'

A Teacher:

Jesus said:

Not what goes into the mouth defiles a man, but what comes out of the mouth, this defiles a man. . . . What comes out of the mouth proceeds from the heart, and this defiles a man. For out of the heart come evil thoughts, murder, adultery, fornication, theft, false witness, slander. These are what defile a man. . . .

And the wise man of ancient time concluded: "Keep your heart with all vigilance; for from it flow the springs of life.

A Stranger:

May I interrupt?

May a man ask a question?

What is the connection?

What mean these mouthings of writings from two and three thousand years ago?

What do they have to do with Good Friday? And what does Good Friday have to do with you? and with me?

You sing that Jesus wept . . . that God loved the world . . . and that God's Lamb took away the sin of the world.

And you talk of a fake fast long, long ago.

And you talk as though we ought to blush at the contents of our thoughts and the directions of our desires!

A Teacher

The Church is saying with new vigor and emphatic language and dramatic action that not only must the sins of the heart be washed away . . .
but righteousness must replace the unrighteousness of poor behavor; and of acquisative selfishness.
Christ's kind of love

blots out the records of the sins of men;
the cheating weight-scale,
bribery in the courts,
the "might makes right" thinkers,
the double standard of morals for men and women,
influence peddling,
beaurocratic advantage taking,
loafing at work or not-work,
situation unethics and new immorality.

But Christ's kind of love does still more.
The Christ who died to take away the sins of the world is the Christ who came alive again on Easter . . . and who *comes* alive in the lives of those who follow him today. And when he gets inside the life, he chases out a whole lot of this other stuff:

unrighteousness
oppression
inequality
disregard for people
starvation
ecological destruction
laziness
tax cheating

stubborn prejudice
and a whole lot more.

Choir "All in the April Evening . . ."

Narrator

We don't know whether it really happened in April. Very probably it was April. What we know we know by faith. We believe it. We build our lives on it. Listen to some parts of the story:

Reader D

Some stood up and bore false witness against him, saying, "We heard him say, 'I will destroy this temple that is made with hands, and in three days I will build another, not made with hands.' "

Yet not even so did their testimony agree.

And the high priest stood up in the midst, and asked Jesus, "Have you no answer to make? What is it that these men testify against you?" But he was silent and made no answer. And the high priest said to him, "I adjure you by the living God, tell us if you are the Christ, the Son of God."

Jesus said to him, "You have said so. But I tell you, hereafter you will see the Son of man seated at the right hand of Power, and coming on the clouds of heaven."

Then the high priest tore his robes, and said, "He has uttered blasphemy. Why do we still need witnesses? You have now heard his blasphemy. What is your judgment?"

They answered, "He deserves death."

Organ "Go to Dark Gethsemane" (Melody line only)

Narrator

The trial of Jesus moved over to the Praetorium, before Pontius Pilate, the governor from Rome. Toward the end of the report of it, we read this:

Reader D

Pilate said to the Jews, "Here is your king."

They cried out, "Away with him, away with him, crucify him!"

Pilate said to them, "Shall I crucify your king?"
The chief priests answered, "We have no king but Caesar."
So when Pilate saw that he was gaining nothing, but rather that a riot was beginning, he took water and washed his hands before the crowd, saying, "I am innocent of this man's blood; see to it yourselves."
So Pilate gave sentence that their demand should be granted . . .
Jesus he delivered up to their will.
And when they had mocked him, they stripped him of the robe, and put his own clothes on him, and led him away to crucify him.

Narrator

They had him do, as was the custom, and carry his own cross. When they came to the place of crucifixion, they nailed him to the cross, and set it up between the crosses of two common criminals. He spoke seven different times. And that afternoon he died while hanging there.

Choir "Man of Sorrows"

Reader A

Surely he has borne our griefs
  and carried our sorrows;
yet we esteemed him stricken,
  smitten by God, and afflicted.
But he was wounded for our transgressions,
  he was bruised for our iniquities;
upon him was the chastisement that made us whole,
  and with his stripes we are healed.
Yet it was the will of the Lord to bruise him;
  He has put him to grief;
when he makes himself an offering for sin,
  he shall see his offpsring,
  he shall prolong his days;
the will of the Lord shall prosper in his hand;
  he shall see the fruit of the travail of his soul and be satisfied;

by his knowledge shall the righteous one, my servant,
make many to be accounted righteous;
and he shall bear their iniquities.

Reader C

Thus says the Lord:
" . . . your hands are defiled with blood
and your fingers with iniquity;
your lips have spoken lies,
your tongue mutters wickedness.
No one enters suit justly,
no one goes to law honestly;
they rely on empty pleas, they speak lies,
they conceive mischief and bring forth iniquity.
Their feet run to evil,
and they make haste to shed innocent blood;
their thoughts are thoughts of iniquity,
desolation and destruction are in their highways.
The way of peace they know not,
and there is no justice in their paths . . .
We all growl like bears,
we moan and moan like doves;
we look for justice, but there is none,
for salvation, but it is far from us.
Truth is lacking,
and he who departs from evil makes himself a prey.
The Lord saw it, and it displeased him
that there was no justice.
He saw that there was no man,
and wondered that there was no one to intervene;
then his own arm brought him victory,
and his righteousness upheld him . . .

Stranger

May I interrupt once again? I am getting frustrated, you know. Apparently you are saying that God looked at mankind, either all of it together or some special nation, and did not like what he saw.
I still don't get the connection. What has all this to do

with Good Friday? What has this to do with an April evening? Are you going to get at it and get with it? Or do I go away again knowing as little as when I came?

Teacher

Friend:
Though I am called teacher,
You, tonight, are pedagogue.
You teach me.
For when you just said God "didn't like what he saw"
You put it just exactly right.
A whole new understanding of Sacred History flashed through my mind.
"God didn't like what he saw!" You are absolutely right!
Still . . . it says another time, he was pleased with men.
It says, of most ancient time,
The blood of Abel cried to him from the ground.
The cries of his people, when in Egypt, rose to his heaven.
God looked, again and again,
And he liked not, again and again.
So he reached down, he came down into the earth in the Person of his Son.
God became man, incarnate of the Holy Ghost in the Virgin Mary
To turn man around,
To change man's direction,
To clear your confusion,
and to die in doing it.

Stranger

Will, oh, will, oh, will you come out and say it? Pleeeeeese?

Teacher

I try, my friend. I try.
The man of whom they read
"He died,"

was Jesus of Nazareth, the baby Mary bore.
He was God.
And no where else will you, or can you, see
a characterization of God such as he.
He was God. And he died.
He is God. He rose and he lives.
Because of him, my debt that he paid is cancelled.
I stand before God today, tonight, purified, therefore pure.
And that purity he not only washed to the outside,
He planted it within for forcing out of me, squeezing out
the prejudice
the selfishness
the unlove
the disregard
the materialism
and every other ism
that hurts the life of man.
Because he died,
having come to do what was not getting done,
I give myself to working for him,
to doing *his* thing,
to living *his* principles,
and invite you to join me.

Stranger

You invite me to join you.
Others have often invited.
I think I get what you say . . .
I get it but cannot handle it.
Some place I have heard a line from your Book:
"Such knowledge is too wonderful for me;
It is high, I cannot attain it."
It is only trite to say, "It's too deep for me,"
and yet it is just exactly that.
You invite me to join you,
To have the bad forced out by the good.
But all I can say is

Give me time, give me time!
Let me think,
Let me try to sort it all out.
It is too much for me to grasp.
My mind cannot handle it . . . not yet.

Choir "Were You There?"
"Jesus in Thy Dying Woes"

Narrator

Before sundown that first Good Friday evening, Joseph from Arimathea had requested, and received permission, to take down the body of Jesus from the cross, and lay it away. The women who had followed him for many months watched, and that evening made their plans and purchases for the final anointing they felt compelled to do.

Teacher

There is danger that we simply feel sorry for the Savior and think thereby we have observed Good Friday.

It is a modern danger, as in Isaiah's age, that we cry:
"Why have we fasted, and thou seest it not?
Why have we humbled ourselves, and thou takest no knowledge of it?"

For this very evening
There are bodies of people once again endangered by riots in our land.
There are freedom-seeking youths frustrated by inability to break out . . .
There are bonds, yokes of oppression,
shackles of inequalities,
stubborn refusals to accept the persons with whom we disagree,
reflected infants and children who will be the uptight youths just a very few years from now,
spiritually neglected children even in the homes of our own churches,
and lonely old people,

and multiple thousands of suffering, anxiety-ridden people of all ages and descriptions in between.

When our fasts begin to include listening to and doing something about the troubles and pains and anxieties of our neighbors . . . then and only then can we expect God to pay attention to our fast; to see it as true and not fake.

Reader D

Jesus said: "Inasmuch as you did it to one of the least of these, my brethren, you did it to me."

Teacher

But there can be no mass movement of righteousness,
no collective morality among men
except of persons caught up by the love, one by one
by the love of him who is the Leader of Freedom.
You see . . . if you are forgiven, you will love him who forgives, and for his sake you will forsake . . . you will leave behind the things that are for you encumbrances to righteousness. You will discard the attitudes and activities that God looked down and saw long ago,
their modern counterparts in your life,
the things he saw and did not like.
All who are forgiven will forgive . . . and forsake . . .

Reader D

Jesus said:
"Behold, I stand at the door and knock. If any one opens the door I will come in to him and eat with him, and he shall eat with me.

Teacher

He came in . . . he lives with us . . . he changes our lives.
He is
The same one who suffered,
the same one who died . . .
and rose.

Choir	"Lord of Life"
	"O Darkest Woe"
Veiling of the Cross (in darkness)	
Choir	"Long Live God"

A Special Service

Going Home!
Barbara J. Foster

Leader

"Come to me all ye who labor and are heavy laden, and I will give you rest."

Response

"Wherever two or three are gathered together in my name, there I will be also."

Reading

I Judge
I Hate
I Discriminate
I Slander
and
Christ
forgives . . .

— Dianne Duncan

Hymn "Dear Lord and Father of Mankind"
Verses 1, 4, 5

Scripture Luke 15:11-24

Readings

Quote from "The Waiting Father"

We listen to the Story of the Prodigal Son at first as if it were an interesting tale with which we ourselves have nothing to do. A rather odd but fascinating fellow, this Prodigal Son, undoubtedly true to life, undoubtedly a definite type of person whom we have all met at some time or other, and certainly we are all objective enough to feel a bit of sympathy with him.

Until, suddenly, our face may change too, and we are compelled to say, "There I am, actually this is I." All of a sudden we have identified the Hero of the tale and now we can read the whole story in the First Person. This is the way we must move back and forth until we have identified ourselves with the many people who surrounded Jesus; for, as long as we fail to recognize ourselves in these people, we fail to recognize the Lord.

"And he said, 'There was a man who had two sons, and the younger of them said to his father, Father, give me the share of property that falls to me.' And he divided his living between them. Not many days later, the younger son gathered all he had and took his journey into a far country," and there he squandered his property in loose living.

I want my own way God
I want what is due me and I want it now
I want the chance to get out and live
I want to be able to do my thing and swing a little
I want to see the world and taste the sweet wine of prosperity and comfort
To be at the right places at the right time
To impress and be impressed and be swept off my feet
To go to a far country to seek fame and fortune
I go to the right university for the best degree
I choose my friends carefully and do all I can to impress them
My home is the best, my clothes the latest in fashion
Everything I have reflects the good taste and highest quality.

"And when he had spent everything, a great famine arose in that country, and he began to be in want . . . But when he came to himself, he said . . ."

I am empty God
I have nothing
I am homesick
Where is the meaning
Love
Acceptance
Help and Guidance

Roots
What I once knew?
I look at myself and am disgusted
I have become a polished and refined fool to be laughed at, pushed around and pitied
and one who could fall on his face
I keep searching for the face of kindness and understanding
I long for love and concern and acceptance
All that I have are diversions
I run from one activity to another to get away from the loneliness.
I remember what it was like to be home
There was love and warmth and acceptance
I didn't have to explain or apologize for my moods or behavior
When I needed to talk it out, I could
I could be me without questions, challenge or false efforts or facades
I was accepted when I wasn't very acceptable
I was loved even when I was a disappointment
I belong there
I want to return
Do I have the right to go back
Do I have the guts to return after all I've done.
— Thielicke

Hymn "O Master, Let Me Walk With Thee"

Beyond the Prodigal Son

What is home?
Is it where our parents are?
Is it where the heart is?
Is it a place with physical features
Can we ever feel really at home? Or, must we wait until we go to our Eternal Home?
Home is where we are
Loved
Accepted
Forgiven

Where we find
Meaning
Roots
Guidance
Help

"But while he was yet at a distance, his father saw him and had compassion, and ran and embraced him and kissed him."

We all know the end of this story that Christ told. What love there must be for the father to wait and watch, hoping his son would return home. How comforting those arms of love must have been to the son who was so uncertain of his worth and the reception he would receive after all he did.

Christ tells us the story. He shows that God seeks us and calls us home.

The ultimate theme in the parable is not faithlessness of men, but the faithfulness of God.

Paraphrase of Corinthians Passage

In Christ, we are called
To deal with men
From a new perspective
For once, we were bound by indifference
Now we are free
To be . . .
. . . aware
. . . involved
. . . selfless
. . . empathetic
We were not at one with God
In thought, feeling or will
We were rebellious
Our estrangement made us captive to ourselves
We were guilty
But we could find no relief
God acted
He was not indifferent
Christ stepped in

To bind up the broken relationship
He did not excuse our sins
But forgave us . . . the sinners
He became selfless
He made himself vulnerable
So that we might
Know the true sense of
    involvement
    concern
    compassion
    empathy

Life Together

"The prisoner, the sick person, the Christian in exile sees in the companionship of a fellow Christian a physical sign of the gracious presence of the triune God. Visitor and visited in loneliness recognize in each other the Christ who is present in the body; they receive a meet in each other as one meets the Lord, in reverence, humility, and joy. They receive each other's benedictions as the benediction of the Lord Jesus Christ; but, if there is so much blessing and joy, even in a single encounter of brother with brother, how inexhaustible are the riches that open up for those who by God's will are privileged to live in the daily fellowship of life with other Christians."

Life Together—Bonhoeffer

Hymn "O Brother Man"

" . . . The joyful sound of festivity rings out from (The parable of the Prodigal Son) whenever forgiveness is proclaimed, there is joy and festive garments. We must read and hear this gospel as it was really meant to be: *'Good News!'* News so good that we should never have imagined it. News that would stagger us if we were able to hear it for the first time as a message that everything about God is so completely different from what we thought or feared. News that he has sent his Son to us and is inviting us to share in an unspeakable joy.

The ultimate secret of this story is this:
There is a homecoming for us all *because there is a home.*"

— *The Waiting Father*

Closing

Go forth into the world in peace; be of good courage; hold fast to that which is good; render to no man evil for evil; strengthen the fainthearted; support the weak; help the afflicted; honor all men; love and serve the Lord, rejoicing in the power of the Holy Spirit. Amen.